*This book is dedicated to my family first,*
*for all their love and support,*
*who gave me the space to transform*
*from an employee to a thriving business owner.*

*This is also dedicated to the amazing tribe of*
*women who are going to read this book,*
*take action, and leave **their** marks on the world.*

# CONTENTS

The $100K Sales Method

Ryann Dowdy

Raymore, MO

Ryann@100ksalesmethod.com

Ordering Information:

Special discounts are available on quantity purchases by corporations, associations, educational institutions, and others. For details, contact Ryann Dowdy above.

Printed in the United States of America

First Edition

ISBN 978-1-5136-9027-8

Publisher: Winsome Entertainment Group LLC

# ACKNOWLEDGMENTS

I have to start by thanking my husband, Kevin.
From the wild ride of getting married and having kids to
entrepreneurship, writing books, and changing the world,
you've been my never-ending support system. I am so grateful.

To Davis and Georgia, thank you.
You're my why. Everything I do, I do to make the world a better
place for you to live.

To my parents, Terry and Ruthie, and my sister Shannon.
I am who I am because of you. I love you.

# FOREWORD

Why did you decide to start your business? Are you here to make a ton of money? Help a ton of people? Change your family's life?

When I first started freelancing back in 2014, I was simply desperate to get out of my 9-to-5 job. Call me naive, but I was shocked to learn that people won't just give you money because you started a business.

I had spent most of my twenties working in various entry level jobs and filling marketing roles for various small businesses. When I became an independent contractor, I knew how to talk about my side hustle in the form of broadcasting my message online from the safety of my Facebook posts. I was freaking awesome at it. But actually talking to real humans about what I did felt super uncomfortable.

Are you also hiding behind a social media content plan and marketing strategy because the idea of selling is nothing short of terrifying?

As a natural marketer, I feel this deeply. And as someone who has learned how to stop avoiding my fear of rejection and failure in pursuit of actually reaching my financial goals, hear this: if you bypass sales, you are guaranteed to fail.

Here's the good news: Ryann's book will teach you this essential skill in a way that is fun, interesting, and totally painless.

I first met Ryann when I was working as the promotion and events coordinator at the Kansas City Star. Ryann was the newest sales rep to join the team. She sat in the cubicle across from me.

In the decade since, Ryann and I have always had friendly banter between us about my passion for marketing and her love of sales.

Here's what I remember most about our time as colleagues: Ryann, and her sales peers, all made, *minimum*, tens of thousands of dollars a year more than I did. And the real gut punch? I probably worked twice as hard (or at least twice the hours).

Don't tell Ryann I told you this, but if you like money and you don't want to work 24/7, sales wins every single time.

Why? Because as entertaining as marketing is, it's the sale that produces revenue. It's the sale that gets you a return on all that marketing effort. It's the sale that helps you help your clients. I so wish I would have understood this in my early twenties, because I could have gotten my family into a better financial situation a lot sooner!

After being self-employed for the last seven years, and a business owner for the last four, and connecting with hundreds of six, seven, and even eight-figure business owners, I can tell you that every single one of them have at least one thing in common: they know how to get people to buy their stuff.

If you want a successful business, you don't need to work harder. A ton of people work hard, but don't have a bank account to reflect it.

You also don't need to rebrand, create more content, or update your website.

The one thing you need to learn how to do that will have a direct (and immediate) impact on your bottom line is **sell**.

If you're ready to stop hiding behind your business and get real results in the form of bank deposits, relax! You've come to the right place.

Ryann's no-nonsense, easy-to-implement approach will give you exactly what you need to become one of the 10% of female business owners to make it to six-figures.

You simply cannot do that without selling something.

Ryann will show you how.

~Lauren Golden
Bestselling author of *The Free Mama: How to Work from Home, Control Your Schedule, and Make More Money*
www.thefreemama.com

# PREFACE

To All the Women in Sales and Those Running Their Own Businesses...

I was you just a few years ago—a new entrepreneur seeking clients that would bring me the success I saw all over the internet. I wanted the freedom entrepreneurship would give me and plenty of coaches and consultants with six and seven figure companies promised me and many other women that they could be self-employed, too.

Self-employed and rich with money, opportunities to work with astounding businesswomen, and to mentor others who had a dream like mine – that is what I wanted. The life I wanted would also include plenty of time for family and personal interests.

Over time, the dream just got bigger and better. I became committed to my dream when I saw all of what it could give me, and I saw that right away.

I wrote this book to help you, a woman business profes-sional, grow your business because I know you can, and this book will show you how. You will learn from my experience of starting my business and making no money the first eight months to *generating over $1 million in sales in less than two years.*

This book will help you avoid the time and mistakes it took me to reach success and show you how to successfully create a business.

This book also demonstrates my move from successful director of sales to a seven-figure boss of my own business to show you how that can be done. Even if you're not a director of anything in your current job, you can leave it and become a very successful entrepreneur.

But beyond that, this book is meant to show you, if this is your dream, too, how to create a business that serves you while deeply serving others – beautiful clients, team members, and collaborators.

And since I'm a woman who attracts female clients, I am writing this book to help other women achieve the success of their dreams, no matter what that looks like.

Know that I have very definite opinions and I shoot straight from the hip. I scream YAHOO from the top of my lungs when you succeed, and I dig deep into my clients' latest resistance or circumstance. I'm not rude, but I tell it like I see it. I'm candid, frank, and totally supportive, all rolled into one.

So, I write for women not just because I am one, but because I believe in their success. I do have the experience and know-how to help them become a success, too. I am all about women having what they want.

And, frankly, I can't write to a 45-year-old white dude, anyway. I have no idea what he's doing in his life or how he runs his business. And I would probably disagree with what he's doing.

With no disrespect to middle-aged white men, let's look at the current hierarchy of business. At the top of the heap are some well-known names – Tony Robbins, Bob Proctor, Brian Tracy, Stephen Covey, Grant Cardone, just to name a few.

I understand how they got there, and I respect the work they have done over the years. Kudos to their success. But we all know that sales, and business in general, has a long history of being run by and for men.

Yes, there have been many women at the top of sales teams, including women of color, but very few compared to men.

To demonstrate the effectiveness of women in business, let me remind you who is at the top of their business careers – not just in terms of sales, but as thought leaders: Oprah, Brène Brown, Mel Robbins, and Marie Forleo, to name a few. They succeeded mostly on their terms. When they speak, people listen, or watch them, and certainly buy their books and products.

There is no reason why women can't create a business that reflects their personality, talents, and points of view. They do not have to be cookie cutters of businesses that men have built.

Yes, Robbins, Tracy, and the others have sold millions of books. They continue to sell out their programs, products, and services, too. They are brilliant, and their success is undeniable.

But I want there to also be smart, capable, successful, and loud female voices in business. There are lots of women who fit this description – I've had more than a few as clients and mentors – and I especially want to see them using sales to grow their own legacy. If they choose, I want them to select a career in sales.

Sales is what ignited and formed the basis of my entire business model. When I was the director of sales at a digital marketing agency and would advertise for a salesperson, I would receive resumes from dozens of male candidates, but zero female candidates.

I found that interesting, but frankly, it made me angry.

I knew women didn't apply because of how the job was described. The words in the job title and job description, plus the reputation of sales being a man's job, is one that often turns women off. All of this continues to do nothing to attract women.

So, for me, my mission is twofold: I want to hold myself up as an example of what's possible for women, and I want to inspire women to be the woman that I describe in this book. They are who I am writing this book for.

In addition to training women in sales, a third important motivation for me is being honest with my own personal brand. My brand is all about empowering women in business. I am focused on their success.

It often starts with smart, capable women not yet realizing they started a business because the work they do lights them up and makes an impact. BUT clients, profits, and a growing company doesn't happen all on its own. Nobody told them sales is the cornerstone of their business.

Selling your services, selling your team on your vision, or rallying your team so you make greater profits, and negotiating with vendors in general, is all a sales activity.

Once you've mastered the sales process, you can use what you've learned to great success in all three of these areas.

## Why I Have So Much Faith in Your Ability to Learn Sales And Be a Successful Business Owner

I would like to put an idea to rest about sales. Often, my clients think that it's just new entrepreneurs who need to get better at sales.

It's been my experience that even more experienced entrepreneurs, people with successful businesses, still don't know sales well enough to either do it well consistently, or be able to train a team to do it.

I have also learned as I work with CEOs that they need sales training, too. At all levels, business leaders need to know how to use sales to grow their companies. I have built an entire business around this idea.

## My Background – Why Start a Business?

I never really thought that I needed to be an entrepreneur. I was in control of my income as a salesperson. After I had my first child, I went back to work as the director of sales for a digital advertising agency – my dream job. About four months in, I thought to myself, *I can't do this forever. I don't want to do this forever.*

What I didn't like about being an employee, after spending fifteen years in sales, was the lack of freedom. It was also knowing that the next step up the ladder meant more travel, more pressure, more all the things I didn't enjoy about the job.

I didn't realize there were other options. I felt very much stuck in golden handcuffs as the breadwinner in my family, making a decent amount of money. How could I make a shift? How could I make a change at this point in my life?

It occurred to me to change industries before it occurred to me to leave and start my own business. Starting my own business did not cross my mind for the longest time.

I thought about working in another industry – it would pique my interest and get me excited again. In the meantime, I started attending networking events. I had spent eight years on the road training sales teams, so I didn't have a local network in my hometown of Kansas City.

What happened next was interesting. I kept meeting women who were starting or running businesses, and they all had super smart, brilliant, and great ideas. But their businesses were often struggling. What was going on? Why weren't they growing?

Typically, it was a sales issue. So, either they weren't selling, or they were the seller as well as the CEO of the business. I met several owners of multimillion dollar businesses who were also the primary revenue producers in the company.

That was no way for them to grow the company. They have created their own golden handcuffs since becoming entrepreneurs. There was nobody else in the business to drive revenue for them. That's when my spidey sense started to tingle and I started educating myself about online entrepreneurship.

My next step was to hire a business coach. I actually worked with Lauren Golden from Free Mama for six weeks. She helped me pull apart my first idea of how to get out of my full-time job. As they say, what you start with isn't always what you end up with.

I spent the first eight months in 2018 working on becoming a career and life coach for 20-something women. That was the first iteration of my business. I felt the need to change how young women presented themselves professionally after I attended career fairs and sat across from them in interviews. I knew that, with instruction and guidance, that they could present themselves in a much more professional way.

This may come as no surprise to you when I say that my personality told me I was the one to show them how to interview better, including how to sell themselves so they could get the job they wanted and start building their career.

I quickly discovered that I was not a career coach. It was not what I was really excited about doing. Helping them build their career was not what really set my heart on fire.

When I thought about what did get me excited, I was not surprised that it came down to sales and teaching sales techniques to women so they could sell their talents and expertise to companies who would want to hire them.

That was what got me excited. I researched sales coaches online and realized they were not as common as general life coaches and business coaches and consultants.

I also found that there was nobody teaching sales techniques or training to new business owners so they could grow their companies. *That was the gap that I could fill.*

I tried to figure out why nobody was teaching it and discovered that people were following the gurus who were not talking about sales because it wasn't sexy. Instead, they were talking about best practices for Facebook lives, or posting to Instagram, or building a big email list by offering a freebie so you can make passive income while you sleep and work five hours a week and make a million dollars a year. (Insert eyeroll here).

That's what people wanted because that's what they were being promised. And I bought into the promise for a while. Needless to say, my entrepreneurial journey had a slow start because I chose to do what all the gurus were telling me to do.

I ultimately realized that those strategies are good and

important strategies, but they're not the right strategies for a new business.

What I mean is, all those things work – content marketing, email marketing, all of it. Anything works, to be honest, but in the beginning days of your business, it's about relationships. ***Relationships lead to sales.***

You can put out all the content in the world you want, but nobody's listening because nobody knows who you are (yet). They haven't met you. They haven't established any KLT – the Know, Like, Trust factor. That comes with time spent getting to know individuals – what they enjoy, what they dislike, what they do on the weekends, what their hobbies and interests are, what their goals are.

Serve people by getting to know them.

Once I went back to the basics, which is going out into the world, networking, and solving peoples' problems, my business started to grow.

To quote Oprah, "Helping others is helping ourselves." I started helping others.

That was late 2018. I made my first thousand dollars in the last three months of that year because I finally figured out that I was not going to get clients by sending emails to the six people on my list.

*~Ryann Dowdy, March 2021, Kansas City, MO*

# INTRODUCTION

## My Hope for You as You Read This Book

My hope is that you, an ambitious woman in business, are the type of entrepreneur who is also passionate about the work you do. I suspect you are since you picked this book out of a crowd of books on business. Thank you and please read on because I think you're going to see a lot of "you" in these pages.

Let's start with this list. Do you see yourself here?

- You are talented and offer exceptional service that helps your clients overcome obstacles and help them transform in the process.
- You admit to having a fire in your belly that drives you to make a big impact.
- While you have the smarts and talents for your work and have had impressionable success in other areas of your life, you're ready for even more. You know that

> sales will take you to the top, but you also have concerns about it.
>
> - Maybe you're never sold a thing in your life and can attribute your current success to your innate speaking ability or use of social media.
> - Maybe you've tried sales and hated it.
> - You may have hired a salesperson and found it difficult to manage them. You didn't have a training program in place and your business turned stagnant and growth slowed to a crawl, or even worse, stopped altogether.

Maybe that's where you are right now, and you don't like it. It doesn't reflect who you are as a person or the goals you have for yourself and your business.

Your goal is to build an empire, be well known. You want to be a legendary and revolutionary businesswoman who holds influence and prestige. You want to be a force in your industry, but need guidance around building the best, most profitable business you can.

Right now, you have so many ideas about how you can help your clients. But you're not yet a household name or at the top of the leaderboard you see in your mind.

You won't be that leader until you've mastered the basics of sales principles and learn how to use sales to bring you from invisible to invincible.

## What I Want This Book to Do for You

This book is meant to demystify the sales process and show you that sales is an ethical and honorable business practice. It is not just the practice of shady used car salespeople. It isn't icky to do, and you will never be disrespected for doing it when you have in mind the best outcomes from the success of your sales. Disrespect comes when someone leads the sale with what they can get in commissions rather than serving their new customer.

It's what has built many businesses and it also doesn't matter who's at the top – a man or a woman – as long as they use the proven tools. Make them your own, add your own language, and take them on, but use them so they feel like second nature.

## How to Use This Book

Learn the sales tools I offer you and understand them. Then put them to use to see how they work and how they will build what you want. But mostly, believe in yourself, your capabilities, and your ability to learn new things. Those new things will fulfill all your dreams, help you hit and exceed your goals, and make you one happy woman.

Guaranteed.

# THINGS NO ONE TOLD YOU ABOUT ENTREPRENEURSHIP

In July 2019, I began my program, Uncensored Sales, and since then, I've achieved more than I ever did working for someone else: a business making a half million dollars in less than 18 months (with over $1 million in total sales), and the development of a dynamic, smart team of creative women employees who are happy to help me build my success while I help them build theirs.

I've trained more than 200 clients and have watched them achieve six-figure and multiple six-figure sales in a year. At the beginning of 2021, I formed a partnership with my mentor, Kelly Roach, herself a highly successful businesswoman. Together, we run the Social Sellers Academy that promises to be an eight-figure per year and beyond company.

What does this all mean? It means I'm creating a legacy for my family – a company that supports our financial and lifestyle needs, happily retired my husband at age 40, and serves the needs of businesswomen who also want their companies to support them in all the ways that are important to them.

I don't tell you this to brag about myself. I say this because I know what the secret sauce of business success is. And I can tell you that it isn't a secret, and it works for every type of business out there.

That "secret?" Sales.

You know what else? Sales = Business Success.

Not websites. Not funnels. Not making Tik Tok videos. Not social media or any other kind of marketing.

Very simply, successful entrepreneurship is a sales job and sales is a relationship game.

Whether you're selling your services, negotiating with vendors, or leading your team, entrepreneurship is the ultimate sales gig.

You may be thinking, *But I can't sell and I don't want to. Salespeople are all about the money and pushing people to buy.*

Yes, we all know about the pushy used car salesman, but sales is more about building relationships than it is about convincing someone to work with you.

Does that sound unbelievable or untrue?

Think for a minute about the things you do every day and how much they look like a sales job.

If you've gotten a job, you've sold yourself.

If you're married, you've sold yourself.

If you can get your toddler to eat their vegetables or tie their shoes, you're consistently selling. It's the misconception of sales as a pushy, obnoxious person convincing you to buy from them that gives sales a bad reputation.

Do you see a common thread in this list? It's the relationships you build between you and the person you are selling to, even if it's your toddler.

What we as women entrepreneurs need to do is totally reprogram ourselves so we view sales from a different perspective than the idea that selling is convincing and conniving.

I talk a lot about that with my clients. We don't spend our time convincing people. Sales isn't about turning noes into yeses through force.

Women business professionals don't realize that to make an impact (which is why they started their business to begin with), they need to build relationships. Relationships are the basis for selling. When you learn the steps in sales, you achieve success.

And guess what? Women are natural born salespeople because women are natural born relationship builders. And I stand by that statement because I see women using their innate relationship skills all the time to build six-figure, multiple six-figure, and seven-figure businesses.

I used sales to build my own business, so I know from personal experience that you can learn how to sell as well as I do, and I challenge you to do even better.

## Forming and Leading Your Team

At some point in your business, when there's simply too much for you to do by yourself, you'll need to put together a team that helps you achieve sales goals and increases profitability. To lead your team to success, you'll rely on sales techniques.

Why? You're selling your vision. You have to enroll your team of employees in your vision. You have to sell that vision to your team every single day.

Understand your team members' motivations. Remind them of their motivations. As the high achievers that they are, you don't need to pat them on the head, but you will need to incentivize them in a variety of ways.

Also, find out what motivates them. Money is not the only motivator. Find out what's in it for them as an employee. Care about their goals and help your team achieve them.

When you understand and honor their motivations, they will provide you with their best selves. When their best selves show up each day, your business skyrockets.

## Negotiating with Contractors and Service Providers

We know that every business needs something in the way of products or services at every level, whether it's a virtual assistant, software, Facebook ads, or an advertising agency. There are 1,000,001 different people that you need to help you run your business. If you don't get really good about negotiation and sales when it comes to hiring, you are always going to be overpaying for those services.

It is impossible to do business in a vacuum. It is impossible to do business alone. Eventually, you are going to need contracted help, employees, legal services, and the expertise of consultants in order to grow your company.

Those service providers have to be sold the concept of doing good work for you consistently. Sales is a never-ending process.

You must sell them on when, why, and how they should work a little harder for you. You must sell them on the concept of offering you a discount because you sign up for a six-month instead of month-to-month contract...and an even better discount when you pay in full for those six months.

And that, as you know, is an important part of growing a business.

Let me tell you a story. At one point in my career, I was in a mastermind group and one of the members had a client come to them and say, "Hey, are you able to give us better terms or a discount because we're a longstanding client that has given you testimonials consistently?"

The woman said, "I don't know what to do. We don't really negotiate, but I don't want to alienate this person. They're a great client. They've been with us a long time. They've given us testimonials. They're huge fans of ours."

A gentleman named Joe, who was also in the mastermind, added his thoughts and said, "I ask for discounts, over-delivery, and extended terms all of the time because I get them. And if you do not ask, the answer is always no."

He went on to say that his asking for a discount did not reflect the value of the service providers' work. It's also not because he wouldn't pay full price. He asked because he could. And you know, if you ask for it, oftentimes you will get the discount or a better deal and your margin increases.

He also went on to say that, no, he wasn't trying to insult anybody. He was just trying to do good business.

This is the lesson from these stories. You need to understand that you are not insulting people by negotiating. You are not demeaning them or anything along those lines. It's just business – and you don't know what's available until you ask!

Remember what he said: if you don't ask, the answer is always no. You must ask with tact, with love, and with the goal of building relationships in mind.

That's my whole philosophy on vendor serviced providers. I ask for better terms all the time because I often get them.

We have no problem asking for an upgrade on a rental car or

a flight, but we have a hard time asking a contractor to work for an extra couple of hours or eke out another email.

Sometimes the answer is no, which doesn't mean we don't see value in those services and those service providers. It just means that we can't take things at face value. At its worst, never asking for better terms actually leads to being taken advantage of.

If you are negotiating something, either with a client or a vendor, and they ask for the discount or the extra time, it may mean a little bit less in your pocket, or it means a little bit more time spent with them. What it also does is create relationships that are better for both sides.

Know this, too: it's easier working with that person because their needs have been satisfied. It's actually a settling point for both sides instead of it being agitation.

We think negotiating prices and circumstances is a bad thing when, no, negotiation is about finding something that's beneficial for both parties.

It's also about understanding business in general. If you're able to negotiate and come to something that's mutually beneficial, you have a client for life, you have a referral for life, you have a raving fan. Reciprocity happens, too.

It's mutually beneficial for the employees you serve and it's mutually beneficial for the service providers that serve you, as well. It's all about understanding the value of human connection and understanding the value of that long-term relationship.

## Selling Your Services

We think online businesses are simply social media, websites, offers, and pricing. Business is sales. None of the other things matter if you don't sell anything.

I'm going to be bold here and quote a famous businessman, Thomas Watson, Sr., who started IBM. He said that nothing in business happens until a sale is made.

You may feel that parts of your business need help – your website is old and your branding is even older.

Rather than hire a web designer, you need to make sales. You can run a business without a website and make six figures in a year. I've literally seen this happen over and over again.

Wait until you have the money and a clear vision of what your website should look like and what it needs to say.

Typically, though, my clients tell me that they forget sales, or avoid sales, and start working on their website or their Instagram content. When I tell them the secret to a successful business is sales, they experience an aha moment. They may even feel silly for spending the time on their website, posting on social media, or sending out emails to their list of 100 people.

Sometimes, they even feel stupid. They'll say, *how did I miss that?*

I can tell you how – through the ads, podcasts, and books, yes, books, that tell them to do all these things.

From there, they start to panic and say they're bad at sales. They say things like, "I've never sold anything. I don't want to sell. I don't want to be annoying. Sales are gross."

You've got the used car salesman idea. You've got the idea that the telemarketer who calls you is trying to pull a scam. You get hit on Facebook with the "Hey, girl!" messages. These are friendly but targeted messages that get you to question what you're doing to build your business and how can you live without this person's course, program, mastermind, or 1:1 service.

That all leads you to frustration and feelings of overwhelm. You know you need to sell, but you're scared to be seen. You don't want to be lumped into that category of pushy people. You and everyone have been conditioned to think that sales is a bad thing.

What winds up happening is you spend an exponential amount of time on things that don't matter to your businesses, none of which is actually helping you create the business of your dreams.

You have this wild misconception of what business is and that all those things are an important part of business. None of them matter if there's no money coming in. If those activities don't save money or make money, they are not as important as making sales.

So now you have to totally pull apart this conditioning and understand that selling is helping people. Selling is serving. And when you view your business as a way to solve problems for people, selling just naturally happens.

Now, let's talk about women and sales.

Guess what? We are naturally great at it. Why? Because of our innate abilities to connect and serve. It's woven into who we are – blame it on socialization, blame it on biology, blame it on God.

It doesn't matter how you've come to be so good at it but think about this – women are more relationship focused. Want proof? Go into any household and ask them who in the family manages the relationships? Who plans the holidays? Who plans the dinner, the outings, the backyard barbecues? Who plans which sport the kid is going to play in and how they're going to get the kids there? I would be willing to bet it's mostly planned by a woman. And it's done because of her ability to connect, serve, and solve problems.

Added to relationship building is another important part of sales: the data.

I always say business is composed of two things – people and numbers.

But here's a funny thing that happens – women wind up going off the deep end about data. It's as though you realize you're great at building relationships and know how important that is, but you focus solely on that and drop the numbers and metrics tracking altogether.

You have to weave those two things together: data + relationships. Business is about relationship building, solving problems, connecting, and tracking the numbers.

Then, when it's time to grow a team, you are selling them on wanting to be a part of it. You are selling them on doing work that some days might be hard, arduous, and tedious.

On the days when they don't feel like it, and on the days when they feel like crap and all the days where, let's say, their kid threw up in the car, or the dog got sick right before work started, your employees have to come to work and be the best version of themselves and be a good steward of the company's funds.

You, as CEO, have to sell to your employees the ability to reframe their day so they show up to work in our businesses willing and able to work every single day. Hiring a team and then rallying the team and getting them to really see the impact that you want them to make is yet another sales activity that you, as the business owner, have to do.

You and I are impact driven. I know that your business is your passion. Along the way to growing your business, you have to get other people enrolled in that mission. And that part can't just be about business. It can't be just about the numbers. It has to be about the people and the numbers.

The ultimate sales job is getting somebody to come to work for you and do good work. You may think, as an employer, that you're paying them and they should just come to work and get the job done. You have this idea that when you hire and pay them, you should just do what you want them to do, including the tasks you've been assigned.

While that will work in the short-term, it will not work in the long term because people do things because of their own motivations, not yours, and a paycheck is not enough motivation for most people. They can literally get that anywhere.

Also, your employees are human, and as humans, they think in terms of what is in it for them. The mistake that a lot of companies make is making it all about what's in it for the company.

Nobody gives a hoot about what the company wants. Nobody gives a darn about the company's goals. They care about their own goals. You want to align their goals with yours for the best outcome.

It's like this: if you can better understand your people's goals and help them achieve those goals and sell them on why showing up and staying late or coming in early, or sending that extra direct message they need to send, or doing that extra thing at the end of the work day – if you can show them that doing the work is going to get them what they want, they will do all of that and more.

If you stand on the idea that you give your employees a paycheck so they have to do whatever you say, you lose in the end. It doesn't create the impact you want to make with your business. It is the connection that helps other people achieve their goals and dreams, whether it's through selling them a service or hiring them for a job in a place that allows them to achieve their goals and dreams. Those are both sales jobs.

You have to solve problems for the people who pay you and you have to solve problems for the people inside your organization. Sales is about solving problems for everyone.

I understand if this chapter has made you nervous. I've talked about sales, hiring, and negotiating. I am offering you all the reasons why not selling is a mistake and why selling is what's going to take you to phenomenal and great success.

And it's an uneasy thing to read. You didn't start a business to do ANY of these things.

What I ask you to do is to look at sales as a business practice, and like any business practice, take the emotion out of it so it doesn't influence your opinion. When you show up timid, it means you're worried about yourself rather than the big picture of your business.

Asking for the sale, talking about money to service providers, engaging your team are things you have to do when you want a business that works for you.

When my clients say, *I couldn't possibly go ask for more money or this person has asked me to discount my rates,* you know what I tell them? I say, "All they did was ask a question. You don't have to make it mean you're not valuable or good enough."

For your employee or your prospect, it's about negotiating

greater value. They are trying to find a mutually beneficial agreement and they do that by asking for one.

If you tell them no, or your prospect tells you no, they don't want to work with you, that's okay.

You don't have to apologize for anything. If somebody says, *hey, can I get this at a lower rate?* It's okay to say, no, the price is what I just quoted you because of the value that I bring. I hope we get the opportunity to work together, but unfortunately, I'm not able to lower the price.

Think about when you are asking someone to discount something for you. You may feel uncomfortable asking for that but know that you're not trying to take advantage of people. You're trying to find a mutually beneficial relationship. And that is, ultimately, sales.

## Worthiness Vs. Value

Let's take a moment to talk about worthiness. I see this in my clients all the time. They judge their worthiness on their ability to build and run their business. If it does well, they're on top of the world. When business slides, they think something's wrong with them and they second-guess their own strengths and instead focus on their weaknesses.

I always say business and worthiness are two separate things. How successful your business is, how much money you make, how much you sell, how big your teams are is totally irrelevant to your worthiness.

You are inherently worthy, right? God put you on this planet for whatever your purpose is and your business, successful or not, does not play into your worthiness at all.

Your self-worth, your worthiness, is not tied into the success of your business. If you see worthiness as a reflection of your business, then you feel good when you're making sales and a great income. You feel terrible about yourself when sales slip, or you've lost a valuable client.

You can't allow yourself to swing up and down from worthy to unworthy based on the swings you see in business. You are always 100% worthy no matter how well your business is doing at any given point in time.

We need to detach those two things to grow a business in a healthy, successful way. You're looking for validation in your business and that's not where validation comes from.

We've gone over the three big sales topics: selling your services, rallying your team, and negotiating with your service providers. We've decided that your own, personal worthiness is separate from business.

This is a great start. When you master these concepts, your focus is where it needs to be. Now, instead of wondering how to build your business, you're actively building your business.

## Sales Always Comes First

I am going to be frank with you here. I'm not many business-women's first investment.

Typically, you've already invested in either coaching or a course and either or both of those got you into entrepreneurship. Once you've laid down the money for the coach or course, you are then told that you will be catapulted into success that allows you to leave your nine-to-five and build a successful business. Bam! And done.

Let's look at this a little closer. Yes, oftentimes that course gives you incredible skill sets: how to be a virtual assistant, how to be a digital marketer, how to be a bookkeeper...the list of possible skills you learn is long.

Maybe you've invested in coaching to help with confidence, improve your mindset, and encourage you to keep marketing.

But then things often go south. It's after six, twelve, sometimes 24 months into your business-building journey, and you confess you're not making any money.

You're more than a little frustrated. You're overwhelmed and you're blaming yourself for your lack of success. You know it means something about you, and it isn't good.

I often hear this: *I am not cut out for entrepreneurship. Maybe being a business owner is not for me. There's something wrong with me.*

When I talk to people who feel like this, my first question is always: *How many new people are you talking to every day?*

Most people know the answer to that question, or they'll start talking about their twelve Instagram followers, or their Facebook group with 56 people in it or an email list with 24 people in it.

My next question is, *what is the problem that you solve for your clients?* In response, I usually hear some kind of "I help . . ." statement. Or they say, *I work with this type of client or that type of client*, but you aren't clear at articulating the problems you can solve for your ideal client.

Honestly, at the beginning of business building, there are exactly two things you need: You need to talk to people, and you need to be able to clearly communicate the problem that you solve for them.

Instead, so many women like you come to me, feeling like they've been an entrepreneur or trying to build a business for a long period of time and do not understand why they're still struggling to get clients.

Of course, you know why, right? It's because the sales piece is missing. You're focusing on marketing, you're focusing on busywork, you're focusing on things that don't actually move the needle of sales. And you don't realize (or don't want to admit) that sales keeps the needle moving forward.

You may say to me, *If I could just sell my way through my first couple of clients, then I'll reach the point where I can do Facebook ads and webinars and launches to get clients.*

You don't want to hear that sales is a never-ending business activity. There is no other way to long term, sustainable business success except through sales.

Whether you're selling or somebody on your team is selling your services, someone in your business has to be selling. Otherwise, there's this giant gap in the business and it looks like a hobby more than a business that can sustain the lifestyle you want to live.

My new clients often come to me with beautiful branding and beautiful websites. They've determined packaging and pricing. All of these are important things, but they're not making any money at all. So, the women lose confidence in themselves.

Oftentimes their family and friends are frustrated, too, and wonder why things aren't going the way their loved ones want them to go. Then women start having deep feelings of despair, of imposter syndrome, and all of this is whirling around in their heads with no relief.

I know what's missing in their business, and yours. You, the reader, do, too. What is it? That missing piece? That gaping hole? When I'm working with that client, I get her to plug into the simple, but often hard to do, concept of building relationships. That is how you start to make sales. Build relationships.

You build relationships by talking to people about them. All the sudden, opportunities appear everywhere because opportunities ARE everywhere.

I would say that seven times out of ten, this is the story women bring to us. It's commonplace, and here's the kicker – it's totally fixable.

When I bring up the word "sales," then a whole bunch of objections are raised around selling:

- It's icky.
- I don't know how to do it.
- I couldn't possibly do it.
- I'm doing all the other things because I was told I could get clients and not have to sell.

I'm going to take a stand here and say that sales can be, but does not have to be, icky. You can learn how to do sales, and sure, those other things will help you build your business, but they are a long game, my friend, and you need the cash NOW.

Let me tell you a story about my employee, Kayla. When I hired her to come sell for my business, she had zero sales experience. And in fact, several times when I offered her the job, she told me, "No, I don't want to do sales. It isn't my thing."

Sound familiar? Then the pandemic showed up and she's working from home. She wasn't happy with her job. I asked her to help me out with some things. And we just started with some softball tasks like engaging and welcoming people to our Facebook community. She's so friendly and personable, I was getting feedback about how helpful she was to members of my group.

Through all of that, I talked to Kayla and said that the only thing missing here is you booking the call and asking for the sale.

I could see a lightbulb go off above her head. She said, "Huh, okay. This is all that sales is?"

And I said, "Yes, absolutely, this is all that sales is – building relationships and solving problems."

Once she realized that, she literally, in less than a year, generated almost a half million dollars in sales, simply by talking to people and building those relationships. And she's excellent at it! She's not pushy. She's not salesy.

I think sometimes she hesitates to tell people that she's in sales because what she feels doesn't align at all with her vision of selling. But what she was really good at, and is still good at, is talking to people, and she is great at connecting, asking good questions, and making people feel safe and comfortable.

And that's really what selling is. We always say that sales is the transfer of inspiration. Kayla's really good at inspiring people and helping them see the potential in themselves and giving them the confidence to invest in themselves. That full circle has made her into an excellent sales rep. We just honed her innate friendliness and now call it sales.

Even as we are changing her job by moving her over to my other business, Social Sellers Academy, where she's selling to a totally different audience, her connection rate is fantastic. People love talking to her because she's so good at making it about them and focusing on the relationship.

Sales isn't hard, as you can see. It's just about having a genuine interest in helping other people through their problems.

# 2

## CLICHE ADVICE WORTH ITS WEIGHT IN GOLD

### Your Network Is Your Net Worth

Yes, it's a cliche to say that your network is your net worth.

But it's so true! Networking, expanding the number of people you know, is essential for sales and business building. You must talk to people in order to know they need something from you, right? It doesn't matter what you sell, connecting with people who may want your service or know someone who does is the difference between running a hobby versus running a legitimate business.

This is what I see with my clients: a constant misunderstanding about the networking process. They think, *I have to be an extrovert. I have to be a people person. I have to live in a different area of the country where people will buy what I sell.* All of that is untrue, except for a few instances, such as living by the ocean if you sell ocean cruisers. Otherwise, your buyers are everywhere.

The same is true for online entrepreneurs. They claim they're in the wrong Facebook groups, or they're talking to the wrong people on LinkedIn.

## Everyone is the Right Person to Network With

But here is a major truth: there are no wrong people to network with. You cannot tell by looking at people, especially images of them online, that they do or don't want to buy from you. You won't know that until you talk to them.

I have sold services to all sorts of people, and the ones I least expected to buy from me did, happily. Do not try to guess their interests from afar, and don't try to guess how much money is in their wallet. Talk to them, find out what they need, and offer your services to them.

When you start talking to people, you're networking! And here's the deal – anyone can network.

You can certainly tap the ones that are easy or have already told you they want your services. These are what I call the low hanging fruit. But you also need to talk to people you've never spoken to before, or don't know well. Have a conversation with them and learn about their needs and wants.

Here's something else to realize, and this is part of why everyone is good to network with: you don't have to talk directly to the person who needs what you're selling. They may have a friend, a family member, or a son or daughter who does. At first, you may decide the person isn't a hot prospect, but when you learn that they know a few people who could use your services, everything changes.

This is what networking looks like. It's just talking to people.

## Stop Looking for Clients and Start Building Relationships

I would love for you to stop looking for clients. I know, pretty shocking, right? Instead, I want you to start doing something else – building relationships.

Building relationships will help you make sales more easily. This is what I hear and how I reply to women that come to me:

"Ryann," they say, "I am networking my face off and I'm just not finding any clients."

And I reply with, "That's your problem. You're looking for clients instead of building relationships."

Relationships = clients.

You know that nobody is walking around with a sign around their neck that says, I have the problem that you solve. The only way that you're going to learn is through actively building relationships.

Focusing on building relationships takes the "ick" factor out of what you may think of when you think of 'sales.' Relationship building takes off the pressure of hunting for clients and pitching them within a minute of meeting them. Relax, chat, ask questions, and listen to what people tell you. That helps you offer them exactly what they need.

I'd like to introduce to you something I call the Power Hour. It's a block of time you take to spend networking. Now, most of you are online, so that means using social media as a place to establish new relationships. You do that already on your Facebook page, right? You respond to a friend's post, and one of their friends likes it, and they reach out and "friend" you and before you know it, you're posting comments on each other's posts. That's networking.

When you intentionally spend time networking, the Power

Hour peels away all the negative feelings that most people have about sales. It's an easy and comfortable way to reach your daily goals of networking with people.

Your focus is to build your network each day. Not only are you going to get involved in way more conversations because you don't have an agenda, but you're also spending your time not looking for something specific. And by something, I mean the exact right person or the exact right post or the exact right thing to say. Your focus is on building new relationships with people.

Now look around you. We are blessed to live in a world where we literally have billions of people at our fingertips.

So, while you know that you can access billions of people, I continue to hear from women who say they can't find their people and wonder why. Because you are all looking for the perfect and ideal client instead of looking to meet someone, learning more about them and what they do, and adding them to your CRM. Networking is all about building relationships.

When you realize that networking is not this idea of there being right people and wrong people to network with – you just think about building a network – then that feeling of there being no clients where you live, or where you hang out online, goes away. That's also when the magic starts to happen.

Everybody knows somebody. You miss an opportunity when you don't reach out to people in your existing network. Again, women say to me, "Well, they're not my ideal client." But you have no idea if your next-door neighbor's niece needs what you do. You have no idea if your sister's best friend's husband needs what you do, but you just think, *will this person right in front of me buy something from me?* And when they don't, you get discouraged.

That's why you don't like or value networking and that extends to why you don't like selling because you look at everybody as dollar signs instead of looking at them as relationships.

Some of those relationships will lead to money.

Some of those relationships will lead to referral partners.

Some of those relationships will lead to collaborations.

Some of those relationships will build friendships.

I will say that at this point in my business, some of my very best friends are women that I have paid to do work for me, or they have paid me in some capacity.

When you stop putting this expectation on networking as a revenue-generating activity, it works for you. I repeat: networking is all about looking for like-minded people, serving those people, and building an increasingly larger network. As you do, all sorts of miracles take place.

I have a specific story about this. One of my very first paying clients was a woman that I met through networking. I met her at a female-based networking organization that I joined, and we decided to chat over a cup of coffee.

At that time, in my head, there was no way that as a sales coach I could help her. But I did know that she knew people I needed to know, and I knew people that she needed to know.

We just had a cup of coffee and we got to know one another, built a relationship, and continued to see each other at events. It was a relationship of, "Hi, how are you?"

Imagine my shock when I saw an email from her in my inbox years after we had met. We had both gone our own ways, but she remembered me, what I did, and reached out to me for help.

Of course, I asked myself, *why would she need my help? She has a successful business, a multimillion-dollar business, and all the things that come with that.*

Here's the kicker. What she actually needed was a way to get out of the primary revenue driver position of her business. She was CEO and her company's main salesperson. She couldn't sustain both positions and she needed help figuring out a sales process step by step so she could eventually hire a salesperson and go back to just being the CEO.

Just through that network, just through continuing to see one another and build a relationship, she came back months later and bought from me.

When first networking with someone, don't worry about whether or not that person has an exact need right now. Or she doesn't fit the exact right criteria as a potential client. Or she has a successful business so she couldn't possibly need your services. Let go of the tendency to make assumptions about people, what they need and what they want and who they know and how you can have that relationship develop.

If you dwell on the idea that they fit zero of your preconceived criteria, you miss the opportunity to build relationships, which almost always and ultimately lead to referrals, collaborations, and sales. But this wrong idea of networking persists, and it remains, for my women clients, something that does not work for them.

This is what I also hear from women like you in the online space – a certainty that networking involves going into a Facebook group and hunting for the exact person, your ideal client. Does this sound familiar? Or you may be the person going onto LinkedIn and sending out a hundred outbound messages.

And while some of those strategies will work, that's not what you're trying to do here. It's just not sustainable or efficient. You're trying to build a network of people. I always say that the more people who know what you do, the more money you will make.

You should also be working on building sustainability long term. That's why a lot of people are afraid of networking. It's a long game. Of course, you can show up at a networking event, meet somebody, build a relationship and close business within a week. That happens all the time.

But we live in an instant gratification world. I always say, when you're like Amazon Prime with same day delivery, get it now, better, faster, cheaper, whatever, you're building a lack of patience in that relationship that does not need to be there.

When it comes to sustainability, think old school calm and patience, and build your list of people. The more networking that you do, and the more people that know what you do, the bigger your business will grow. This is what pays your mortgage, your car, your dream vacation. It will pay continuously, too, in 90 days, six months, nine months, years and years down the road. Trust me on this.

Here's another great story. Just recently, I got an email from a woman named Erica Brown that I met when I was pregnant with my daughter, Georgia. As of right now in 2021, Georgia is two.

Not surprisingly, Erica and I met on a coffee chat, and I remember sitting there super pregnant and mad about having to drink decaf coffee. That was literally the last time I saw her in person. We were connected and friends on social media, but we hadn't been doing any sort of business together, chatting, or hiring each other over the last few years. Really, we were just friends on Facebook.

I got an email three weeks ago from a woman I had never met named Christine. In her email she said, *hey, I had a conversa-*

*tion with Erica Brown, and she recommended that I reach out to you, Ryann, about sales training.*

You see what's going on here? Erica and I have not spoken in nearly two years after meeting each other at my favorite coffee shop, catty corner to my actual office. But Erica knew me and when she was networking with Christine, who mentioned she needed help with sales, whose name came up?

Specifically, Christine said in her email, *I need to talk to you about sales training. We just hired my daughter to do business development for us and we don't know how to train her.*

Look who she reached out to – me! Here's the lesson yet again. Had I gone into that coffee chat looking for instant gratification, thinking to myself, *what can this woman do for me now,* (or what is this going to turn into today), I would have left that café deeply disappointed.

But here we are years later and she's connecting me to people, which is just wild. This is the magic. People come back when they know, like, and trust you, and you have services that are easy for them to "sell" on your behalf.

Let's look at networking from the angle of ultimate sustainability. It fills your pipeline forever and ever. If social media blew up tomorrow, the people that you know would become your sole business ecosystem, right?

If Facebook were to go away, Instagram closes, or LinkedIn dies, your network doesn't die with them because it's sustainable. It will outlast social media. It will outlast whatever trendy thing comes up next. You could say, your network contains your ultimate relationships.

Think about your network of contacts: other moms, other wives, friends, and neighbors. They are your network, too. You form networks all the time – helpful people, or just people you've met who you may call on in the future or may call on you when they need help.

You need to know the referrals you get from the networks you are in are vetted. You may be meeting the referral for the very first time, but there's a trusted middle person between you two. It's still a cold call perhaps when you chat, but you've been vetted, which also means the referral is already excited to talk, and possibly, to work with you.

Think about your business network as helpful people. You are part of their network, so you're potentially helpful to them.

It's all the same thing. Know that you've created and continue to create a personal network. Now flip your thoughts to a business context. Your business contacts? They are a network, too.

The other awesome thing you're doing during networking is building the "know, like, and trust" factor that is key to landing clients. Trust is especially powerful. When you can say to someone you may have recently met, or even someone you met a few years ago, something like, "I know someone who can help you with that," the person you're talking to sits up and listens.

When you do this, you're overcoming all the behavior that skeezy, stranger salespeople do on the internet. What you're doing is creating introductions from inside your network.

Here's something else that's amazing: when people see you on social media and they see all the people in your network, that impresses them. *Wow*, they think, *I wish I knew that many people. I would be totally successful if I did.*

They also think you must know something they don't. That you're smart. That you're a success and know what you're doing. Now, that's a perception, but the people who perceive your success consider it a reality.

You start to look like an influencer. Believe me when I say that the people you're connected with on social media, the circles of people that you run with along with the master-minds or group programs that you're in start to see you as influential.

Remember, it's a perception, but to them it's real.

## Anyone Can Network

People (maybe you?) think that networking is for extroverts. That networking is for people that live in major metropolitan areas, for people that sell business-to-business services, not busi-ness-to-consumer services. Networking is for people who sell expensive things. Networking is for people who sell services and not products.

You may have this image of who an avid networker is. And you often describe her as an extroverted salesperson who talks too much and is someone you really don't like very much.

You have to change that mentality about introverted people. You need to know you can be an excellent networker because networking is about relationships. Introverts are amazing at building relationships!

And, sure, as an introvert, you might not like being in a room full of 200 people. But you can build excellent relationships when networking one-to-one or in small groups.

You have all these ideas about networks, but I like to pull it back to this single, important idea: It doesn't matter who you are or what you do. If you genuinely want to connect with and help people, you can find a way to network. And whether that's in person, whether that's online, whether that's through small networking groups or big networking groups or paid networking groups or free networking groups. Pick one way, or all the ways, but just do it.

When you take sales out of networking and just focus on relationship building, it doesn't matter what personality type you have, or socioeconomic status. It doesn't matter geographically where you live. If you're just seeking to build relationships and trying to help people, know that you are just meeting new people. That's it.

Also, do not believe the people who tell you it just doesn't really work in their industry because it does.

Alright, I admit there are exceptions. Some industries, including high C-level Fortune 500 executives, or doctors and other healthcare professionals. There are a few other industries, but I would say 98% of all industries benefit from networking. What you do instead is not look for opportunities to network but look at an industry and make assumptions about the people in it. That's called storytelling.

I had a conversation with a woman named Carrie once who wants to get into social selling and leveraging social media for her CPA firm.

She had chatted with an acquaintance, Susan, who thought of herself as a sales expert. Carrie told Susan that her ideal clients are tech companies, agricultural companies, and home construction services. She also told Carrie that she wasn't active on social media, but that she would like to get clients through social media if she only knew how.

Susan told Carrie that considering her types of clients, she wasn't going to find clients on social media because social selling doesn't really work. Susan then informed Carrie that the only way to get in front of her ideal client was through cold calling.

Cold calling isn't my favorite, but don't get me wrong. I've grown several multimillion-dollar sales organizations through cold calling. But there's this misconception that you can't use social selling for some industries.

There are more people with a smartphone than there are people with a toothbrush and those smartphone users are online. Everybody uses the internet, especially tech companies, agricultural companies, and construction firms. They may use it differently than we do, but they are on the internet doing business.

For instance, they might view Facebook as a business tool. Let's take a roofer. They are one of the industries she serves, but her thoughts were telling her that roofers are not found on social media. They are busy people installing roofs.

Yes, but they are also on social media when they're not installing roofs. Plus, it's often not the installer that you're targeting, but the manager or owner of the company. Of course, there are roofers on Facebook, and especially, LinkedIn. Social media is a great place to find your ideal client. They need to network, too!

Today, you're an exception if you don't leverage social media for business. We always think we're the exception. We know our people. We know what services they buy, but somehow, we also know, falsely, that networking online and certainly selling online is just not going to work for us. And I have pointed out the true exceptions to the rule – calling on doctors, and top of the line C-suite executives. Otherwise, there's no one and nothing that networking can't get you in front of, and social media is a great place to network.

Let me add this: if you're networking in the right place, you can get in front of the doctors and C-suite execs, too.

My girlfriend sends her kids to private school. She and her husband made the decision to educate them privately because they wanted them to have an education that includes religious instruction along with the academics.

But what she underestimated was the network of parents whose kids are also enrolled at the school. She has met other moms and dads who have opened up all sorts of interesting business opportunities for her, and for her and her husband.

She's gotten in front of some C-suite executives, and she's gotten in front of people who have millions of dollars in venture capital. She has also gotten in front of people that have sold businesses for millions of dollars. She and her husband didn't know this when they placed their children in the school, but they discovered an amazing network of new friends and amazing business contacts.

And so, again, we don't think of those things that are outside the realm of business when we think of our kids' school or the P.T.A or the sports organization that we joined as a family, but these are networks, too.

You don't think of the barbecues. You attend church each week, but don't think of it as a place to network. You don't think of preschool pickup as a place to meet other parents. You don't think about where your kids go to school and the activities that bring families together in service of the children and their school.

You totally miss those opportunities as networking opportunities. Which is where you can get in front of pretty much anyone. Lots of people you want to meet have kids!

My husband went to a Catholic high school. Let me tell you about the network of people he knows. First of all, he sees and knows someone from his high school everywhere we go. He also knows their backstories and their personal lives.

He tells me about a business his classmates' parents started. We'll drive somewhere, and he'll point to a business and talk about his classmate so-and-so's buddy who now owns it. Then there's the people who have taken over that car dealership from their dad, and so and so has taken over that flooring company. My husband knows them all because he went to high school with them or their relatives.

This is a huge network. Yes, it's a bunch of people who attended his Catholic high school, but they're business owners and buyers of business services and products. And they are always happy to help one of their school's alums. Everyone knows someone they can introduce you to.

This is what a network looks like.

## Stop Looking at People as $$ Signs

Looking at networking as a way to get clients is not the best approach. Please stop looking at people as dollar signs and start looking at them as relationships. Now let's talk about the concept of there being no wrong people. Okay, yes, you need to be in a room full of business owners if your clients are business owners. If you work with moms, you need to be in a room full of moms.

But that's not the issue that people are having. Instead, they serve moms and think their ideal client isn't in the mom group. Or the entrepreneur group doesn't have the right type of entrepreneurs in it.

You can see where I'm going with this. Networking is about meeting people who can help you grow your business. If, along the way, one or two of the people hire you, that's great! But more likely what happens is that your network is going to refer your next client or introduce you to someone they know who is specifically looking for your services.

That's what I mean when I say there are no wrong people to network with as long as you are in the right room.

I think that's an important point that a lot of women business owners miss. Let's think through the concept of the 'right room.' Whether it's a Facebook group, Instagram, or in person, if you sell to entrepreneurs and you're going to mom groups, then yes, maybe you're in the wrong room. But think this through some more. You never know who in that mom group knows an entrepreneur, or may be one herself, but doesn't talk about it in the mom groups on Facebook.

Let's not always assume you're in the wrong group, but instead use some logic here. You want to do everything possible to get into the room where there is at least some semblance of an ideal client there.

But once you're in that room, there is no wrong person to build a relationship with. Because if they're in the entrepreneur group, they're in their mom's room, or whatever room is YOUR room, the people you are meeting there have networks as well.

Don't be the person who's looking for the sign around the neck of the person who has the problem that they solve. It happens like this: you walk into the room, shake a hand or two, and unless the people need your services, are super excited to introduce you to someone who does, or is just excited to meet you in general because you're awesome, you decide those people aren't your people.

This happens a lot when it comes to networking. We're looking for people who are looking for us. We're waiting for people who are advertising in some way that they need us. Maybe they are on social media saying, *hey, I'm looking for a virtual assistant.* Or maybe they're in a mom's group saying, *hey, I'm looking for a sales consultant.*

Maybe they are on LinkedIn saying, *hey, I'm getting ready to hire a copywriter.* We spend our valuable networking time looking for those opportunities where people are actively saying, "Hey, I'm in the market for _____," instead of spending our time creating opportunities.

## Creating Opportunities, or Becoming Known Before You're Needed

Let's talk a minute about creating opportunities because this is key. Creating opportunities is the concept of becoming known before you're needed. There's a lot of people in the world that don't necessarily know that they need your services.

They might not even know that a particular service even exists. I always like to tell the story of when I started my business, I didn't know virtual bookkeepers were a thing. I assumed that I was going to have a CPA or an accountant local to me manage my books.

I had no idea that I could find someone on the internet who could virtually do the day in and day out bookkeeping in my business. The first bookkeeper that I hired was somebody who was already in my network. I never went to a Facebook group and announced, "I need a bookkeeper." I had one in my network already.

Beyond bookkeeping, I've never announced in a Facebook group that I need a social media manager, or a Facebook ads manager. These people were already in my network. I got to know them, added them to my network, and when I needed the services they provide, I hired them. That's the whole idea of becoming known before you're needed.

Because again, they might not know that you exist. They might not be ready for you yet. They might not have known that working with someone like you was even an option.

When you're thinking about networking as this whole idea of finding people that are looking for you, you're missing the relationship building piece. My goal is to not go into a Facebook group looking for the person who offers what I need. I don't suggest that you do, either. First, think about your network. Who, of the people you know, does what you want?

Whenever I need help, I go to my network. I am involved a mastermind full of seven figure entrepreneurs. I don't go out to the general public because I don't have a relationship with people there.

I like to tag my network for help first. If I don't know someone who offers what I need, I will contact someone in my network who does. I appreciate their referrals and if they have worked with the person, that's even better. Then I know that I'm getting someone who offers quality services. I still talk to them and see if we can work together, but it's a much easier process to just tap my network for help.

This matches the data that says 60% of jobs are never actually posted on job boards. Hires are made internally, or someone in the company refers someone they know for the job.

In my experience, I would say 90% of business opportunities are never actively advertised. You belong to a mastermind, a mom's group, a group of seven-figure earners and someone in your group, which is a network, will have someone for you to meet, or knows someone who does. And even better, that somebody is already in your network and offers exactly what you are looking for. Use your network to build relationships so you can serve them, and they can serve you through services they offer, and give referrals to people who offer what you need.

Networks = opportunities, friendships, resources, referrals, and introductions.

<u>Know, like, trust.</u> We've talked a bit about this before, but networking is such a great example of how this plays into building, not just a group of people you know, but a trusted, helpful network of people who are interested in your success because they know it will come back to them.

Your network may be your mastermind friends, or your BNI connections, or your high school alums from back in the day.

My point, and I just can't emphasize this enough: you are going to trust the referrals you get from your network. Building the know, like, trust factor is one of the best and biggest benefits you get when you build your network.

## Coffee Chats Make You Money

Let me tell you how I got my very first paying client back when I first started as a sales coach. I was on LinkedIn, and I connected to a gentleman named Gary, who I discovered loves sales as much as I do.

In the meantime, a woman posted on LinkedIn that she was looking to connect with other female business owners. Gary tags me in this post and says, *I don't understand how you two have never met. You're both powerhouse women in business and you two would benefit from a conversation.*

So, of course, we took Gary's advice, and booked a coffee chat.

I learned that Sarah lived not that far from me, and in the course of our conversation, she mentions that she designs websites. She told me that she works specifically with speakers and authors.

Then she asked me what I do, and I told her that I was building a sales coaching business because I found this giant gap in the market. No one, at that time, was teaching sales to women coaches and service providers.

Sarah then tells me that she never knew there was such a thing as a sales coach.

"I suck at sales," she said, "Can you help me?"

And on that coffee chat, I sold her a one hour session on Zoom.

She loved it and picked up what I was teaching her quickly, so she extended our work together for several months. This took place years ago and she still refers people to me. This amazing client came from a networking relationship where I met Gary and he referred me to Sarah, and I got a new person in my network who also became my client.

Remember how I spent a good part of 2018 drinking coffee (decaffeinated coffee because I was pregnant the back half of that year)? And my second office, cattycorner to my actual office, was the local coffee shop. It was a quiet, perfect place to meet people, and I did. I met tons of people there and established, as you can see, many long-term business relationships, and a few personal relationships, too.

The amount of business I did in that coffee shop probably made the owner wealthy! But seriously, so many people used it as a meeting place. I was not alone in that at all. Coffee shops are the perfect place for a coffee chat.

I think back to those times of meeting people and drinking

coffee and smile. I spent a lot of time with people I didn't know, and it was the best possible thing I could have done.

Kudos to the owner, who got to know all of us who met at his shop and bought a ton of coffee! The shop had a friendly vibe and that actually helped make it a great place to meet new people.

When I get a reaction from female CEOs who tell me that coffee chats are a waste of time and having coffee with strangers is not useful or why networking without any qualification of the buyer first, I think back to how successful I was with coffee chats while I was a corporate employee, and later when I started my own consulting business.

Here's something else that chatting with a lot of people can do for you. In addition to building your network, you can use the time to practice talking about your business.

If your business is relatively new, or you struggle with sales, or you struggle with talking about what you do, coffee chats are a great low risk way to connect with people. It goes a long way toward building relationships that will get you clients.

So, I think that arguably a coffee chat, or whatever you want to call meeting with people, is one of the best things you can do along with being the best use of your time, especially if you are an early stage entrepreneur, early stage salesperson, or your calendar is not booked with sales calls and client work.

As your business gets bigger, or if you're a sales rep, you will start to book actual sales conversations. Early on, coffee chats are a great way to practice talking about your business, figure out the verbiage that people use and learn how people react to what you say or the questions that they ask. There's so much value in those networking conversations.

## What Coffee Chats Look Like When Your Business is Bigger

I just launched a second business in partnership with another businesswoman. She brought up my need to get back in the game of networking. But the networking I will do today as compared to the networking I did when I first started my business is basically the same except for the type of person that I will invite for a coffee chat.

Our ideal client is a seven or eight-figure business owner. They're a coach, consultant, or run some type of service-based business.

They're ambitious and already successful. Their needs are different from a startup in terms of how they sell. I am selling them on building a sales team so their workday isn't about selling to keep the business growing. Their time is too valuable for that. For the company to grow, they need to bring in a sales team.

They have other team members: copywriters, designers, maybe a COO or at least an OBM. Yet, sales is often the weakest part of the business, which is why they continue to do the work. What they actually need to do is step back and give the sales job to a dedicated salesperson or team member.

In my job as a partner of this new business, I get to do something I know how to do quite well – sales. Like you, I continue to network with individuals and in some cases, I network in group settings. I've practiced my sales message, but I continue to find that talking to the people who would benefit from my program helps me fine tune what I say. Talking to them also allows me to hear their issues so my partner and I can improve our program for them and others after them. What's different in this new business is the actual conversation. It's about how to help the CEO of a high sales organization continue to grow in the best way possible.

Your network, the people that you can call by phone, send an email, or shoot a text message to, is invaluable. If there were a secret sauce of business success, your network is it.

Networking allows you to create a (digital) Rolodex of contacts. You then fill it with great resources, collaborators, and yes, clients. Remember that you can continue to grow your contacts because you're lucky to live in a world where you have access to billions of people. Start networking now.

3

# HUSTLE IS NOT A BAD THING

Hustle Versus Hustle Culture

Let's talk about hustle versus hustle culture.

The concept of hustle is being dragged through the mud now in the entrepreneurial space. There are so many people out there telling you that you can build a business without having to hustle. And I just want to clarify the difference between the hard work that defines hustle versus hustle culture and burnout.

We need to talk about this because there are a lot of people who say that hustling is a bad thing, when the bad thing they're really talking about is creating a nonstop work life that becomes part of their company's hustle culture.

That's the vibe I want to address. I want to be very clear that this is not about burnout. This is not about a lack of self-care. This is about working hard to change your life and to change your legacy and to make the impact that you want to make. And quite frankly, if it were dumped in your lap or just given to you on a silver platter, you wouldn't appreciate it.

Let's look at lottery winners. We've all heard about how the majority of lottery earners wind up bankrupt within five years. It's because they didn't have to become the person who makes millions of dollars. They didn't have to put in the time and effort. The money was just dumped in their laps, and they piddled it away. They made bad decisions because they never had to work hard to make that money, so they didn't value it or treat it as the byproduct of their hard work, their hustle.

We have this world full of people who just don't like or understand the concept of hard work because they think that hard work automatically leads to burnout. That hard work and hustle are the same thing.

Hustle = Hard Work

Hustle Culture = Burnout

Let me explain.

In the beginning of building your business, it's going to involve a little bit of hustle. You're going to have to move quickly. You're going to have to try a lot of different things to figure out what works best for you.

But when I say hustle, it can be, but I don't necessarily mean, more hours. It's not about working 60-hour or 80-hour work weeks, pushing yourself into burnout. That is not what I mean by hustle. The definition of hustle is "energetic movement and activity."

People always talk about the hustle and bustle of big cities, and we know that means lots of movement and activity. Transfer that concept of busy movement and activity to your side gig, which transforms that gig to a successful business. That business gives you an exit ramp from your nine-to-five job. Now you're building a six-figure and beyond company.

In the midst of building this business, you're going to have some busy movement and action, and there is nothing wrong with that. I want to tell you that that is a very normal part of building a business.

Now, there will come a time in your business where it is no longer about hustle and it is about building your team. It is about giving yourself more space to think instead of more things to do, but in the very beginning, and I mean in the zero to $100,000 sales range, you are going to have to do some busy movement and activity.

I talk a lot about failing and failing fast in your business and being willing to try a lot of different things that create some of that busy movement and activity. That is how you learn what works and what doesn't. You determine if running a business works well for you. You see if you like working with certain kinds of clients. If you really like networking on the social media platform. If you really enjoy offering 1:1 services or prefer offering group programs.

You learn that by going out and taking action. Hustle and hard work are part of building a business. My friend, I want to remind you that entrepreneurship is not easy. And if it were, more people would do it because frankly, there's a lot more money to be made building your own company.

Let me be clear – there is such a thing as burnout. There is such a thing as too much energy focused on achieving goals at all costs. But there is a difference between the hustle you do to grow your business and buying into the hustle culture.

When I say hustle culture, I am talking about the idea of

working around the clock and never resting or taking care of yourself.

I fully believe that you can build a business in just a couple of hours a day, which most people do who are also growing those businesses while working full-time jobs. During those few hours, however, you are working hard to achieve success. Those couple of hours are consumed with your to-dos, follow ups, emails, billing, sales, and all the other things that make your business successful.

## If It Sounds Too Good to Be True, It Probably Is

When you're hustling, and working hard on what you love, you can bring on a state of flow. Flow occurs when you're passionate about a topic or activity. Being in flow means you're doing work that you're really good at and really passionate about. Time flies by when hours feel like just minutes. You are so wrapped up in that work you love, you want to do it all the time. But know that you can be in flow and still hustle hard. I know this because I can recognize when I'm both hustling and in flow.

For me, flow looks like me being passionate when I'm serving my clients, or when I'm putting out podcasts, videos, and social media posts that I know that people are going to love.

I don't think that hustle and flow are on opposite ends of the spectrum, as much as it is marketed to be – you are in flow, which is good, or you're over there hustling, which is bad.

What I object to is the concept of your business growing before your eyes because you spend all your hours in flow. You're not doing any work, just thinking about the success you'll have when clients sign with you, or seats in your group program fill.

What will get you to the sales levels you need and fill your program is not flow all by itself. It's when you are working hard.

When I think of flow, it is me working my business, which I totally love, and I'm in a bit of hustle time, which is hard work, and time flies by. See the difference?

So, I do believe that you can hustle and be in total flow. Flow looks like you doing work in your business that you enjoy. It looks like you when you feel passionate about the work that you do, or the impact that you want to make, or the direction that you are driving yourself, your family, and your dreams. Some or all of this may also include a little bit of hustle, a little bit of busy-ness, and that's a good thing.

In the hustle, you're often creating that flow energy. And that's what attracts the right people to you. That energy and excitement that has you thinking, *hey, I'm in flow because I love the work that I'm doing.*

You're working hard and loving it because you're seeing all sorts of great things showing up in your world: great clients, great sales, and lots of opportunities to grow. That working hard part is key to growing your business. Do you see how that's going to attract way better people to you than being chill, putting your feet up, and relaxing to "see how it goes?"

You want to create a big business. You want to change your life. You want to change your financial situation. You want to take back control, and to do that, you can be in flow, and you can hustle without burning out. You are in flow by doing work that you love.

I heard Gary Vaynerchuk on his podcast talk about people who are passionate about their work. He described that it looks like jamming out on business. That passion in non-business owners looks like hours on the golf course. Or for others, passion may be a vacation on a tropical beach.

What he was saying was basically this: we don't tell the golfers that they're golfing too much. Or the people on the beach that they're spending too much time there. Or tell the tennis players that they're lobbing tennis balls around the court way too often.

What about the three hours you usually spend on social media, engaging and talking to people because it's fun for you? Or spending time balancing your checkbook, or analyzing data from a huge survey you sent to clients? Are those activities too much of a good thing to be jamming on?

Hustle is also about being intentional with the time that you have. So, my friend, do not be ashamed, do not be embarrassed. Do not worry if you feel like you're hustling now, because again, you're going to hustle your way to 100K, and then you're going to be able to hire a team and you're going to be able to really get into your zone of genius and stay there.

So, just to be perfectly clear, flow is great, but flow without hustle is . . . maybe not the best use of your time if you want to also grow your business. Unless flow moves the needle on your business success, call your flow time a passion. Please don't confuse the time you want to spend in flow with the much needed and sometimes required time to hustle. Also remember, that "hustle" is hard work and from hard work comes success.

## Everything Worth Having Is Worth Working For

This is the absolute truth.

Again, people have this idea that building a business is easy. Typically, this thought comes from being a smart and focused person. I suspect my readers, including you, came from success in some area of your life.

Think for a minute at what you've achieved, even if you've just graduated from college. Were you a successful athlete? Did you win academic awards? Were you voted Most Likely to Succeed your senior year in high school?

Most people who pursue careers in sales or entrepreneurship have had some level of success. That allows you to think that starting a business from scratch or learning a new skill should be easy.

You are also influenced by what you see on social media. Your favorite business celebrities make it sound like they achieved their success and wealth in a minute. You often see the Instagram posts with photos of their lavish trips or them standing in front of their 20,000 square foot home.

It looks like they are running a million-dollar business working three days per week. You are not seeing the behind-the-scenes view of what they have done to achieve this level of success or how their overnight success was fifteen years in the making.

When you are a beginner, hustling is required, and it is required because you are a one woman show. You are chief cook and bottle washer. You do all the things. You are the salesperson. You are the marketing person. You are the fulfillment person. You are the tech person. You are the finance person. You are just one person. If you want to run a successful business that makes money, I don't see how you do that without a little bit of hustle.

Another great word for hustle is grind. You are working and going through the grind, but nobody likes that word. It feels negative. When you say it, it feels in your body a little heavy and not quite right.

Quite honestly, that is the reason why not everyone is an entrepreneur.

But let me repeat myself – when you are growing a business and taking complete and total control of your life and your income, dare I say that there is going to be a little bit of hustle required. Anybody out there who is telling you differently is, I hate to say, probably lying to you.

The reason why I can say that with confidence is because over the past three years, when I started my entrepreneurial journey and even when I had my first inkling that I wanted to be a business owner, I started networking and talking and watching and studying people. I became successful by starting as a beginner and doing all the things it took to create a six-figure business. I hustled.

That is the reason why some people go to work every single day and let somebody else hustle and grind because it is not easy. It is not easy, and it's not supposed to be easy. Nothing in life worth having is easy. All those people that you see who have a certain amount of talent and money and experience and expertise that are collecting checks without working very hard are doing that because they hustled in the beginning.

I like to think of this as a short-term sacrifice for long-term gain. When I decided to start a business, my husband and I had a conversation about it. And I knew that it was going to require hard work.

When I made the decision to go out on my own, I was the director of sales for a digital advertising agency. I had a six-figure corporate career. I was the breadwinner in my family. Leaving my job wasn't simple for me.

I couldn't just quit my job and pursue entrepreneurship. I had to match my corporate salary before I could leave that job.

So, I had to hustle to make that happen. My life looked like a pregnant me working 50 hours a week while I chased a toddler. I was an active member of my church. I was trying to maintain some level of friendships and a personal life. And so the only way that I was going to be able to build a business alongside all of that, my friend, was to hustle and move as quickly as possible, to get it done.

Here is what happened because I was willing to hustle.

I started my company in 2018 and in its first year, I struggled. I think I made maybe $3,000. I spent a lot of time getting ready to get ready.

I then found out I was pregnant with my daughter, Georgia, who is two years old at the time of this writing. I knew I had to figure everything out and make this business work.

I felt like I had limited time to figure it out. If I didn't want to go back to work full-time once this baby was born, then I needed to start hustling. And so 2018 was a total flop. I lost money, maybe generated $3,000 in revenue, and spent way more than that in coaching and tools and technology.

By hustling in 2019, I managed to pull off $118,000 in revenue in my business. Granted, I was spending a lot of money. I was putting a lot of money into my business. Please don't misunderstand that whenever somebody shares those six-figure sales and revenue numbers with you that there aren't business expenses involved. Everybody's got to pay taxes. But it was $118,000.

And I made it. I was able to do it in twelve months while having a baby, and that did not happen without a little bit of hustle. I could have taken the advice from gurus out there on the idea of flow and going with the flow and not working too hard. I could have let clients come to me and stayed in positive energy... (insert eyeroll here).

I hope you can hear the sarcasm in my voice, because I think that is total B.S. The people who get it done, the people who are successful, <u>are the people who are willing to hustle.</u>

That means they are willing to work hard. I've said this before so please don't misunderstand me. I don't mean hustle as in working 80 hours a week. Yes, in 2018, I was working full-time at my job, and then working every spare moment that I had in my business. But once I was able to leave my job and just work in my business full-time, I didn't work a crazy number of hours.

In fact, I work fewer hours now than I did in the corporate world.

For those of you who want to make a couple thousand dollars per month, that's okay.

But if you are chasing your dream and want to build an empire that's a six-figure, multi six-figure, or seven-figure business, you're going to have to work more than twenty hours a week early on. Eventually, you will get to a point where you'll make enough money to hire people and build a team.

Here's the truth: when I was growing my business while pregnant, I never thought that everything felt great all the time. In fact, it never, ever, felt like it. I did not feel physically great. I was carrying quite a load, physically and mentally. But I decided to make things happen. I had to be willing to do it even when I didn't feel like it.

That is what hustle means. It may mean something different to you. Maybe I misunderstand what they are saying on the internet about the word hustle. But for me, that's what it means. It means showing up. It means putting in the work. It means working early and late and really making your business work for you.

And again, if you must grow a business alongside a full-time job, or maybe you are a stay-at-home mom and only have a few hours a day to dedicate to your business while your child is napping, or something similar, you're going to have to hustle in that time.

Building my business meant that I had to rush on the weekends to buy the groceries, do the laundry and try to have friends and go to barbecues. I rushed all the time. While you are hustling as an entrepreneur, you will feel some of that urgency.

At the end of the day, you are building your empire. If you are willing to put in the work, if you are willing to hustle for a couple of years, what you can do as an entrepreneur, earn the amount of money that you can earn, and the impact that it can make is exponentially higher than it is for someone who is working for somebody else.

I don't mean to vilify the need for employees. I have employees, and I love them with all my heart. So please don't misunderstand me when I say these types of things, but there are people that are not willing to work as hard as it takes.

Working that hard looks like true freedom to me. If you put in that hustle for just a couple of years, it will pay off over and over and over again. Believe me, I know this from experience. I was a commissioned sales rep, selling radio advertising in Orlando, Florida when I was 21 years old.

I knew a thing or two about hustle even then, and did hustle, but I promise you, I wasn't making the amount of money then that I make now. And I was working so much harder.

To me, hustle is not a bad word. Hustle is what it takes to win. Hustle is what it takes to get ahead. Hustle is what it takes to build your dreams.

4

---

# SALES BEFORE MARKETING

When I tell my clients that sales come before marketing, I get a lot of resistance. Why? Because we hear all the time that when business is slow, or you're first starting your business, you should start marketing.

But hear me out on this – what does marketing create, ideally? Sales. So why not just start with making sales?

## Marketing Versus Sales – What's the Difference?

Let me tell you what is required to grow a business and what actually moves the needle. I have a story for you.

Before becoming an entrepreneur, I worked for a marketing agency that offered digital marketing and advertising services to small and medium sized businesses, primarily in the retail space. In about three years, we were a $4 million company selling marketing, but we did not do our own marketing, and when we did, we did not do it well.

Our website literally got next to no traffic. We posted on social media, but we tracked our clients, and none of them were coming from social media marketing.

Our marketing was coming from our sales team, from referrals, from existing clients, building relationships, and networking. Let me remind you – in three years, we were making $4 million in sales. That's because we had a successful sales team in place.

So, while we sold digital marketing and advertising, we succeeded primarily because we had a strong salesforce.

What this demonstrates is a common myth, this huge misconception, that marketing grows your business. No, my friends, it's sales that grows your business. What you need to figure out is your marketing message so you can sell it like crazy. Not market it like crazy. Sell it like crazy.

Don't misunderstand me – when you figure out your marketing message, I'm not suggesting that you not brand yourself, figure out your brand colors, design a logo, and hire a web designer. No offense to branding experts and web designers. They are important, but not until you have sales that can pay for them.

There's something interesting that happens on the way to affording websites, branding, and other marketing "tools." Your brand and many other aspects of your business will define themselves over time.

The second myth is that we have to have all these things figured out: messaging, ideal client avatar, all the things in advance of actually selling ourselves. We think we need to be perfect before we can start selling. We need to be on social media. We need to have a website. We need to have an email list. We need to have a funnel.

We need to have all these things and then we can start getting clients.

Here is something else: we are taught that we can get clients without ever talking to them, or that by posting on social media, sharing videos, creating stories on Instagram, we will get clients.

Well, you can, but it's going to take a long time. And most people will quit before it works.

The lack of survival of online businesses (or businesses in general) typically is because people are waiting for marketing or social media to get them clients. They think that they just post on social media, and they will come.

It just doesn't work that way anymore. It did in the beginning. Maybe you remember Facebook when it was new. Your organic reach was amazing.

You could just post on social media and all sorts of crazy good things happened. You were seen, shared, and business came to you.

When business pages were added to Facebook, you would see incredible engagement and the numbers of people who saw your posts increased quickly and steadily.

But today's market is so saturated and so inundated and today's consumer is completely marketed out.

I heard a podcast recently where the guest said that almost 90% of consumers will tell you they don't like advertising.

So, what we are told by the experts is to do a whole lot of stuff that consumers don't like instead of just meeting them and solving their problems.

Marketing is essentially, for lack of a better word, lead generation. It's your brand in the marketplace. It's a very important part of building a business. However, as somebody who sold advertising and marketing for 15 years, all the marketing in the world will not make you any money if you cannot convert those leads to clients.

Marketing is you standing with a megaphone, shouting at people, and hoping that somebody is listening or paying attention.

In contrast, sales is going up to somebody, shaking their hand, building a relationship, and solving a problem for them.

That is fundamentally the difference between the two.

In a perfect world, they work together. They are two sides of the same coin. They are both necessary.

I once did a podcast interview with somebody, and she referred to marketing and sales as roommates. They live in the same house. They're not dating. One can exist without the other. You can be a fantastic marketer and make $0, or you can do no marketing, but instead, go out and make sales that build a $4 million organization in three years by deploying basic sales strategies. Which do you prefer?

In a perfect world, marketing and sales work together. You have a marketing department. You have a sales department. You've got marketing cranking out great content. They're building a brand for us. They're helping us become well-known, and they're generating leads. And then sales is taking those leads and converting them to sales.

That is the perfect scenario, which brings us to the second topic in this chapter: *Marketing Takes Time.*

## Marketing Takes Time

Building a marketing engine is a long-term investment. Marketing is a long game and business in general is a long game. But you are going to get so much farther, faster, by going out there and talking to people. Otherwise, they don't know what you do or know anything about you, and they don't care.

That is really what marketing is all about. It can take weeks, months, even years to create a brand that people know and recognize and refer to and all those different things without actually talking to a person.

Marketing is the constant drip of information.

Now, let's say you're going to a networking event tomorrow. You meet someone, go out for a cup of coffee, you chat, solve their problems, and sign them as a client. They haven't read your content. They haven't seen your website. They may have seen your business card and if your branding is good, and notice that, but this is all they've gotten to know about you until you sat down and talked.

That's the beauty of sales.

One other thing about marketing is this: it changes quickly. How you market your business today will be different, guaranteed, to how you market it a year from now.

I currently run two companies and since starting my first one just a few years ago, the marketing tools available have grown. I feel like I'm playing a totally different game from 24 months ago.

Now, I must be on Clubhouse. I have to be on Instagram, on LinkedIn, and on Facebook with Facebook Lives, every day.

Just two years ago, I could carve out my little corner of the internet and make it work. So, just to be clear, I love marketing. I sold marketing for 15 years, but it is a long game. In fact, our agency rule was to not take clients who wanted to reach a high level of sales in a short amount of time.

If we did, it set unrealistic expectations. They would say, "At the end of 30 days, I want our sales to triple." Unless we were taking the business from another agency and they already had an engine that needed to be fine-tuned, we would pass on them as a client because we were building the marketing engine.

Know that marketing is the train that drives your business. It is also the train that takes forever to get going. It starts slow and builds on itself. In my last job, if someone wanted to market their new company and do zero sales outreach, but also wanted cash flow back in their pocket within 90 days, we would not take the business.

With marketing, you need reach and frequency. Your prospects need to see your message between twelve and sixteen times before they ever interact with you. We know that today's consumer has an attention span of less than seven seconds.

If you are early on in your business journey and you don't even know your ideal client, your message, the problem they have, what keeps them up at night, then you're just guessing what to say in your marketing.

So not only is this a slow-moving train, but marketing on guesses is like throwing spaghetti at the wall to see what sticks. Maybe you can wait until it works, but maybe you also need to pay your mortgage and eat today. You will never be able to leave your full-time job if all you're doing is marketing your business.

In an ideal world, the marketing engine is being built while the sales engine is taking off. Marketing is a steam locomotive and sales is a super-fast bullet train. That describes the difference between marketing and sales.

THE 100K SALES METHOD

## You Can Grow a Business Without Marketing, but Not Without Sales

Let's say I show up for a meeting with your sister. You explained that she needed some help, and would I please set up an appointment to meet with her.

I love meeting people, so I set up a coffee chat, solve a problem or two for her, and she signs a $10,000 contract with me without ever having left the cafe where we're meeting. The referral to me was a big help – I was instantly vetted by you, her sister. Add to that my offering solutions to her problems. Top that with a huge conversation about how she can make positive steps forward in her business.

What this also means is that she's never gone to my website or checked out my social media. Neither my website nor my social media would have encouraged her to contact me and let me know she wanted to work with me in my VIP program. She would not have been an instant sale. Why? Because my website and social media aren't sales tools, they're marketing tools.

Sure, they would demonstrate some of what I'm all about and make her comfortable when she met me, but they would not have closed the deal.

Back in my days working for the digital marketing and advertising firm, our clients would complain to us that their marketing wasn't working.

I would ask them, "Tell me about that, because according to this report, we made your phone ring 92 times last month, and you say that none of the calls bought anything."

That told me they had a sales problem. Their marketing was terrific, but not their sales. Proof that you can be an excellent marketer and still make $0.

So, you can grow a business 110% just through referrals, without marketing. I don't recommend that, but remember, that's your bullet train. You are going to achieve your sales goals much faster by focusing on one person at a time.

You're cruising along on the bullet train and the locomotive steam engine beside you is trying to grab a group of "just the right people" who will want to work with you.

Your steam engine will help build your audience, help you build an email list, and help you grow. Right now, there are just passengers on the train. You're watching what you're doing, forming opinions, reading, and watching your content. What you want to do next is pull them into a conversation, build relationships. *Nothing, nothing, nothing beats human-to-human connection.*

While nothing beats the human-to-human connection, if you are the CEO of a successful six or seven-figure business, how does this apply to you? You can generate all the leads in the world, but if you are the only person who's actually talking to those leads, booking sales calls, and converting those clients, you've never actually experienced the freedom that you wanted when you started doing it.

Often, the bottleneck in your business is you. And here's something else CEOs are not aware of: there's probably an extra million dollars in your existing audience. If you would actually go build relationships with that audience, instead of just yelling at that audience through marketing, you could capture those sales.

Even if you sell to 1% of those people who already buy from you, or you message your followers on Instagram, and build relationships with them, you will increase your sales.

But instead, today's marketing tells you to pop them into a

funnel, give them a recorded webinar, and appeal to all their emotions to sell them all the things.

Then you run them through a five-to-nine email sequence. And if they don't buy in automation land, if they don't buy in that funnel, you never really try to sell to them again.

You shrug your shoulders and say they fell out of the funnel, but they're on your email list. You send them an email once a week, but imagine how much more business you would get if, after they went through that funnel and they landed in your Facebook group or followed you on Instagram, you actually spoke to them.

Reach out, invite them to a phone call and say, "Hey, we're so glad you're part of this community. What's going on? What are your goals?"

You can only overcome so many objections in a recorded video.

Chet Holmes, author of *The Ultimate Sales Machine,* tells us at any given time, only 3% of our market is actually ready to buy. So, if you're looking at a 3% conversion rate on that automated funnel, what the hell happens to the other 97%?

You pray that your weekly emails are compelling enough that they will give you money.

But remember, marketing doesn't sell. It generates interest, but it's not like a sales call to someone interested in what you do. When you hold back on relationship building, you lose potentially millions of dollars.

You may have wonderful Instagram followings, Facebook groups, email lists, LinkedIn connections, podcasts, and listeners that nobody is talking to. Gosh darn it, your marketing is good. You're present every day.

Which is why today's consumer complains that they are

teched out. They're so funneled out and touched out and marketed to that you underestimate their potential interest in what you offer. You think people don't want to be sold to. You say you don't want to bother them. That they don't want a sales-person in their inbox.

But they need to hear from you, especially if you're selling a high ticket consulting service.

Your clients have so many options. Look at wine, which can be a cheap or expensive thing to purchase, but unless you're an expert, buying is a guessing game.

You walk into the liquor store and look around. How do you know the quality of one bottle from the bottle next to it?

I buy wine, and when I do, I appreciate the owner who walks over and explains to me the difference between the many different wine choices they have on the shelf.

Instead of assuming I want to buy the cheapest bottle, the owner will ask me what kind of wine I like, select a couple for me, and guide me through the buying process.

We don't do that because we don't want to bother people. Which is code for not wanting to face rejection. We would rather hide behind our email lists.

This is so key, and women especially need to hear this.

I do think some of it goes back to this idea of how we're socialized as women. It goes back to dating and marriage proposals. Men are supposed to propose. I'm not saying I agree or disagree with that, but we are conditioned and socialized as women to wait and be asked.

This also goes back to the statistics that show women need to feel qualified to apply for a job. But that's what you think you're doing with your marketing. You're just showing people that you're qualified for the job. You're hoping that they call, email, or give us their credit card without us having to show why we're qualified for this job.

I sold marketing for fifteen years, but it's borderline irresponsible as a business owner for you to invest what you're investing in advertising when you are not also building relationships with the people who read or watch your advertising.

You recognize the formula that's being taught: sending out an email once a week, dump people into a Facebook group, and do weekly Lives. It's such a good marketing practice that I'm seeing it trickle into the corporate space. I get more and more invitations to webinars from software companies. Their secret hope is to run the webinars and sell their products and never have to speak to even one person about it. That would be magical.

The problem is this: the statistics show us that if you get a thousand people in a room and you close the typical average of 3% to 5%, you're looking at 30 to 50 of those people.

What about the other 950 people?

Sales. That's how you get those other 950 people to buy from you or to even consider buying from you. That is the difference. I propose you do both. It's not marketing or sales. It's both.

I'm not saying don't run the webinars and the live launches. They are theatrics, a great show. We watch them and decide if they're interesting and engaging. Can they solve our problem?

We watch for all those things, but the conversion comes in relationships. The initial 30 to 50 people that are going to buy from you do so because they were in the market anyway and your webinar got them excited.

They were in the right place at the right time. The other 950 may buy from you a year from now.

Here's a really good story that demonstrates this.

My husband, Kevin, talked me into buying the family a car. We did all sorts of test drives and settled on buying the Hyundai Palisade.

We had the deposit ready to pay when Kevin decided to buy a new house instead.

I know. A dramatic shift in purchase decisions. But we put the car on hold and bought the house.

My fifteen-year-old stepdaughter is about to turn sixteen. She just got her permit and needs a car. We plan to give her one of ours, which means sometime in the next 90 to 180 days, we are going to need a new family car.

Remember, last year we looked at and selected the car we wanted, but now nine months have passed. In the first 30 days after we test drove the cars, the sales reps called us back to check in. They also sent text messages and an occasional email.

That was the first 30 days. After 30 days, the emails, messages, and phone calls fizzled out. We've not heard from any of the reps since then. That means we don't have a salesperson to return to. We must start all over. That's such a wasted opportunity for that car dealership. Somebody didn't bother to stay in touch with us because we didn't buy it within 90 days after test driving the car.

That's exactly what we do with sales and marketing.

*Oh, well,* we say, *they didn't buy it within nine days of watching my webinar. So, they must not be a buyer.*

Instead, we put them on our email list. I still get emails from the car dealership, but my sales rep no longer texts me messages, makes calls, or follows up with me.

It just means that when you go buy a car, you're going to have to buy from somebody else. Which means what that guy did a year ago is gone.

THE 100K SALES METHOD

That to me is the difference between sales and marketing, right? Marketing gets you in the door. Marketing gets the low hanging fruit. The people that were already ready to buy.

Here's a random fun fact about buying that car. So, we were going to buy a Hyundai. I was a Hyundai driver years ago. I've owned three. But my sales rep stopped following up with me. So, there is a lost opportunity post-sale as well.

Because once we sell something to someone, we put them on the sold list and they get the marketing emails and all the automated follow-ups, but no personalization.

But imagine what happens when you stay in touch with that person. It doesn't have to be often. It doesn't have to be excessive. It doesn't have to be salesy. It's a handwritten note. It's a quick text message. It's a "Hey, how are things going?" because that's what creates loyalty between humans. We just want to be seen, heard, and understood.

Real estate is a perfect example of this. Kevin and I have purchased three homes and used three different agents to buy them. Our first agent was just okay. Our second agent was lovely. But my third agent became a good friend of mine.

She's someone I see all the time, day in, day out. We have a relationship. She knew at one point in time that we wanted to live in the neighborhood that we live in now.

But before we moved into our current home, we lived in a neighborhood where, after several months, construction took place across the street from us. These were townhomes and rental properties. We knew that marketwise, we needed to sell our house soon because the value of our home was going to decrease based on all the rental properties being built.

Our realtor was there for us. She was that person I talked to every day. We were friends. We went to the same church. Our kids are the same age. It was a no-brainer to buy our current home from her.

When we are made to feel that way – like a friend and valued customer – then we're loyal. When we are treated instead like a number being pumped through a system, we are always going to buy based on convenience or based on the last person we talked to.

What I see happening is a lot of businesses working really hard to generate leads. But then they are not willing to do the ongoing sales work to actually build relationships with those leads. They dump them out of the funnel and send them out on their way to someone else. Think about that. If you're not giving them a reason to buy from you by showing them that you care, or you're being treated more like a number than a person, then people will buy from someone else.

# 5

## MINDSET FIRST

There is a concept called "mindset" that is spoken about a lot in the online space. Coaches often position themselves as mindset coaches: they help their clients grow their companies, overcome resistance to making profits, or even start a business. They are not exclusive to business. Mindset coaches also help people lose weight, improve their marriages, build a life of their dreams, and more.

Really, they help their clients turn around their thinking about anything that's holding them back or keeping them stuck. There are mindset coaches for every topic niche and for any area of interest.

For you, as a business owner, what exactly is mindset, and how do you use it to build your company into one that helps you earn a great income while having fun? I'm talking about the true, real fundamentals of how your brain works and the science of your thoughts. This is often not discussed.

Read on to learn how you can use mindset concepts and a

few other things to see a huge difference in your business growth and profitability.

## The Power of Your Brain and How Your Thoughts Create Your Results

When I came into the entrepreneurial space, there were a lot of people saying mindset, mindset, mindset. I remember thinking *What does that mean?*

I thought it was just positive thinking. And then when I learned what it really is, I then understood why it's talked about so often.

Let me tell you a few things first. In the corporate world, where I started and built a six-figure career, mindset was tied with tangible results. Even our performance reviews were tied to results.

We were always told to have a good attitude, to do what we were told, show up, and produce sales.

It was always very tactical and complete with tangibles and deliverables. Now, I love all those things. They are very important. And frankly, they are how businesses make money. If we don't focus on tangibles, we're in trouble, however, nobody really teaches us what it means.

We think it's just this persona that we put on when we walk into the office – gotta have a good attitude. Gotta be a good teammate. Gotta be a good employee. Gotta smile and nod at the right times.

Looking back at it, all this talk was a form of manipulation. If I just do the right things and say the right things and stroke the right egos, I would be seen as a good employee and everyone would be happy.

That's what your management wants – reliable, successful employees with great attitudes.

Maybe if you're lucky, you work for a company that does some decent leadership training, which may touch on mindset, but with regard to sales, sales training concentrates on sales – the tactical aspects like acquiring hot leads, determining who's a great prospect, and closing the sale.

What isn't discussed in corporate sales is why two people can do the exact same activity and get a different result.

It's because of their mindset. That's not discussed because in corporate it's all about doing – making more phone calls, following up with more people, adding more coffee chats to your calendar.

These are all valuable things to do. Go ahead and attend a networking event. But if you show up with an attitude of, *I don't like this, or I suck at this,* nobody's going to buy a thing from you.

You will often see it show up in the online space as *I'm in the wrong Facebook group.* Or *nobody wants what I sell. Nobody sees value in what I have to offer.*

In the online space, it can also show up as scheduling more coffee chats, following up with contacts, and scheduling more dates at networking events. All good things to do, but how you show up mentally is what's going to make you successful, what will turn the chats into sales.

Let's talk a bit about your energy match. It's about the energy you use when you approach a task. If you keep running into people that are broke, don't have any money, don't see the value in what you do and are looking for a deal, your energy is not matching the energy that's going to help you win sales in your business. But oftentimes this is the energy you have when approaching sales. It matters what you tell yourself and think when it comes to performing as a salesperson for your business.

You just learned to go do the things and follow the checklist without checking your energy. How many people do you know who just love a good to-do list? Who just loves checking items off a list?

I will admit that I love a pretty planner and all the tools that help me feel productive, but as with everything, how you mentally approach your activity is literally the difference between success and failure.

You can read this book, go on and read all the sales books, and you can listen to all the sales podcasts. You can be the most excellent executor of sales activity and still not make any money because it's always mindset first.

In the corporate world, that was never talked about. In the sales department, there was even less talk about mindset. Instead, we were constantly managing the numbers. Now, just a heads up: I am going to talk about metrics in a later chapter because metrics are very important, so don't think that all you have to do to make sales is have the right mindset.

You also need to look at your metrics to figure out where your mindset is not working. Look at the metrics to ask where the breakdown is in your success? Where do you not believe that sales work is important? Where are you not showing up? Where's your energy not matching the activity that you're doing? That's what you use the numbers to score, not to decide to make more phone calls or attend more networking events.

Employees are taught things like having a good attitude, being a team player, showing up on time, going above and beyond. You're asked to dress for the job you want and not the job that you have. You're taught to find a mentor, offer mentorship, or find somebody who has the job that you want and figure out how they got there. You are told that that is the trajectory for success. These are the things that you must do to be successful.

But what you did not talk about is the power of your brain and the idea that, literally, your thoughts create your results and how two people can take the exact same action and have a different outcome based on their thoughts and their energy.

Corporations do not teach you that. They don't talk about that. You're just told that a person has a bad attitude or that person is not a team player or that person is negative, but you're never really coached on mindset. You are told to not be negative, to be more positive, but I don't recall ever in my corporate career being asked how to think instead.

Even now, as my business partner and I are building out the sales training organization, we're literally bringing in a mindset coach to speak to members of the Social Sellers Academy because we must fundamentally change the members' thinking. Sometimes, it feels like I'm talking about mindset until I'm blue in the face, but the fact is, if you don't believe that anybody is going to buy from you, they won't.

It is that giant gap in your thinking that leaves you oftentimes struggling. When you jump into entrepreneurship, you learn quickly that there's an entire mindset skillset that you haven't mastered. And it's arguably one of the most important things.

Soft Skills: Listening, Empathy, Behavioral-Based Selling Are
Still Not Mindset

Listening, empathy, and behavioral-based selling are all important things to learn, and I learned them when I was in corporate
sales. This is as close as we got to mindset. We would never drill
down into the idea of how you think about the work that you're
doing, whatever it is you sell, and how those thoughts were
literally dictating our results.

I've said it a million times – entrepreneurship is the biggest
personal development journey you will ever go on, but it's not
recognized in the corporate world. You're not really encouraged
to do personal development work because your job is to serve
the corporation, not yourself.

You were encouraged to take continuing education, but it
centered around training that would help you be a better
employee. Companies that had training departments offered us
sales training. Eventually, I led sales training organizations and I
spent years in the field on sales calls. I was always about tactics
and strategy.

It's a loss for corporations to think this way. If they placed an
emphasis on personal development, they would have happier,
more productive employees who would serve the corporate
goals with greater energy and interest. And they would retain
employees and not make them all leave to go out on their own.
If employees saw the positive effects of being a good salesperson
– the income and bonuses offered – they would want to continue
to better themselves while creating a secure position with the
company.

You have to consider more things, like soft skills, that are
beyond tactics and strategy. It includes who are your closest

friends and colleagues. Like motivational speaker and entrepreneur Jim Rohn once said, "You are the average of the five people you spend the most time with."

But in your corporate jobs, you don't have choices about who you spend the most time with. The corporation says, *Here's your office. These are the people that you work with. These are your coworkers. These are your colleagues.*

You're encouraged to get along with those people no matter what. You are discouraged from talking to one another and often wonder if that person next to you is even capable. Are they negative? Are they a jerk? What energy do they bring to the job?

You have an identity shift to make, but the people around you are going to affect your success by encouraging you to think less of yourself and discount your training, drive, and innate talents.

That positive identity shift is hard to achieve if you continue to be around people who are negative, don't believe what you believe, think what you're doing is ridiculous, think that you're never going to make it online, and think that people who make a lot of money are bad. If those are the people you continue to support, or you surround yourself with, then that is what you will continue to see in yourself and your life.

In 2017, we built a house. We moved twelve miles from our old house to our new one. It was not a big move at all. We also had a newborn, and while our house was being built, we lived with my mom for about eight weeks.

We were twelve miles away from our people and that twelve miles, combined with having a small child, a job, and everything else, can actually be far away. We unfortunately lost contact with the people that we had been spending a lot of time with.

Kevin and I experienced this. It was never an intentional

decision to end the relationship with our old friends and neighbors. It wasn't by design. It wasn't because we didn't like those people or anything like that. My husband and I just drifted apart from them.

At this time, I was growing a direct sales business doing in-home wine tastings. I went to wine camp (our annual sales conference), and it was the kickstart that got me back into personal development. I started listening to books and discovered podcasts.

With our house complete, we moved in and found a church that we really love. We both actively serve in that church. My children have been raised in that church. And since we have made that shift, we also turned over our entire friend group, literally during the same timeline that my business became a success. It coincides with the timeline of our move, wine camp, living with my mom until our house was built, and settling into our new home.

In that timeframe, I became an entirely different person. No disrespect to those people, but I don't know if I would have been able to accomplish what I had if we had never moved.

My old friends had been in my friend group for ten years. They were my friends when I was single. They were my friends when our priorities were very different. They saw me as that person and that's who I showed up as. My new friends saw me differently.

When I got into a different space where nobody had a preconceived notion of who I was, I got to become who I wanted to become. And through that change, I have dramatically changed my life in a very short period of time.

I also feel that that's what happened to us during the 2020 shutdown. We got relegated to our homes. I feel like I emerged six months later as a different human because that was the time-frame in which my business took off. That was the timeframe in which I hired my first full-time employee. We up-leveled in a major way in that time.

When I left my first house, I kept thinking, *oh, gosh, now I've got to operate in a different way.*

It's just so interesting to me how we act and are as people when we hang around the same people most of the time. I don't think that the people in our lives want to hold us back. I don't think they want to be jerks. We were all living in our own operating reality. But what you will find most of the time is this – people who hang out together operate in the same reality. When you've been out of that operating reality, and you realize that you get to create that next version of yourself, that's when it happens. When you're no longer under the influence of the group.

I saw that happen for me (and again, no disrespect to those people). It's not that I don't love them. If I ran into them today, I would have a conversation. There's no bad blood. It was just that they saw in me someone I no longer wanted to be.

Instead of deciding what I wanted to be seen as with my old friends, which would have included explanations and hard feelings (friends often don't want you to become someone else), my circumstances allowed me to make new friends, and I got to decide how I wanted to be seen. And I wanted to be seen as somebody different than the old me both personally and professionally.

We made a choice. We wanted a new house. We knew that we loved the idea of new construction. And if we moved that twelve miles, we could get new construction at a fraction of the price. None of these things were by design, but the results were mind boggling.

I feel very fortunate today that 97% of the people that I interact with on any given day are business owners that have the same mindset. They have normalized the idea of making tons of money whereas the rest of the world believes that making a lot of money is impossible.

I get on a mastermind call every Thursday with people who have million-dollar businesses. I just qualified for the millionaire call in my coaching program. There are millionaires everywhere in my world.

People who don't have money think that if you make more, then they will make less because you're grabbing more of the pie, as though money is shaped like one, which it's not. And if there's 1% making all the money, there's nothing left for the 99% at the bottom. No, there's plenty to go around. You generate it. It's not like there's a quantified amount. You create more. You are your own treasury department.

All these thoughts of "not enough" came from the people that I surrounded myself with early on in my entrepreneurship journey, and I used to be one of them.

I tell a story in one of my podcast episodes about the G-Wagon, which is the super swanky Mercedes SUV.

Never in a million years have I, nor my husband, thought of ourselves as luxury car people. Now that I'm making money, I see a G-Wagon on every corner. I'm not there yet when it comes to buying one, but I now know it's possible. More than possible. I'd say that two or three years, even twelve months ago, I wanted to know who spends $140,000 on a car and how did they do that?

This is related to driving through neighborhoods with large

homes. Why would somebody need a house like that? How can you afford to cool it and furnish it?

That was my point of view then. That was the room that my mind lived in. One of doubt, not of wonder and anticipation that I would own a house so big it would be a problem cooling and heating it, or even furnishing it.

Once I moved into a different room mentally, my whole world view changed. Now I live in a house that is probably embarrassingly large. And guess what? We heat and cool it just fine, and there's beautiful furniture in every room.

That is all about the whole concept of what becomes normal to you. When you are constantly surrounded by people who are underperforming, who are struggling, who are having a hard time, who don't want to get better, who don't want to better themselves, who don't want to make a lot of money, who think that sales isn't a good career... when those are your people, that's what you get.

## How to Get Control of Your Mindset

Do you have control of your mindset? We've talked a lot about mindset, and we've talked a lot about what it is and what it means, but what I've realized is often missing from mindset is the how-to. I always found that very frustrating because I am a very type A personality. I like checklists and I like being given the playbook. I will execute on the thing I'm reading.

What frustrated me when I learned about mindset was that nobody was talking in a way that made sense. Instead, it was all about controlling your thoughts. Stop being negative. You've got to control it. And I wondered, *what does that even mean?* Our brains have the same thought many times during each day. How do you retrain it?

I will share what has worked well for me. I typically will reference the work that I have studied with Brooke Castillo as a member of her Self-Coaching Scholars program.

Brooke came up with the Model and it was my first understanding about mindset and how we can control it. The Model has worked well for me. First and foremost, it's about understanding the thoughts that you have and how your brain loves efficiency. If you have the same thought over and over again that it is hard to make money, then your brain just automates the thought, like it's not even popping into your consciousness. Your brains jump into efficiency and these thoughts go on autopilot.

The first thing that you need to do is to identify the thoughts that are keeping you stuck. Brooke calls it a "thought download." You can call it journaling. You can call it meditation. But the first thing you do is get quiet and figure out what you are thinking that does not serve you.

Ask yourself how you feel about money. How do you feel about sales? How do you feel about entrepreneurship? Then write the word sales on the top of a piece of paper.

Over the course of several days, start documenting your thoughts. When you read the word "sales," what do you think? What comes to mind? If it makes you anxious or you'd rather not think about it, know that many of your thoughts are on autopilot.

You may have started thinking sales is spammy because you used to get telemarketer calls in the middle of dinner. Or you're thinking about the pushy guy who sold you your last cell phone.

Many of you don't realize that you hate sales because you remember your parents talking about this sleazy car salesman that lived across the street. You don't even know where the thought came from, but the thoughts feel like a fact. The first thing you must do is understand your thoughts through journaling. When you see the word "sales" now, and you agree that you automatically think, *it is slimy* or *it is spammy*, then this is a thought, and it's optional. You have learned through this book that sales can be an overwhelmingly positive experience for sellers and buyers.

Let's say that trees grow in the ground. Now ask yourself, *Is this true?* And you know right away that of course it is. It's verifiable, and everybody would agree it's true because it's a fact. That's the difference between facts and our thoughts. When you grab onto a thought, it feels factual because you feel so strongly about it.

Here are some common thoughts:

*Sales is spammy. Sales is bad. Making money is hard. Nobody likes salespeople. Growing a business is hard. Getting clients is hard.*

These bring up such strong emotions combined with stories you have made up about them that you can only think these negative thoughts as real and factual when in truth, they are not.

Even though you've thought about this many times, one person can think that getting clients is hard and another person can say, *oh my gosh, I've got clients, I've got so many clients. I don't know what to do with them all.*

That means your negative thoughts are optional. The first thing you have to do is examine thoughts like these and decide: Is this true? Is this factual? And if it is not, you need to shift the thought or you need to dismiss the thought.

I am at the point where I don't need to find a new, better

thought to replace the one that says *having clients is hard*. I'm just not going to think that at all. What I'm doing right now is connecting with new people to try to get clients. That's awareness. Ask yourself, is this getting new clients thought easily true or false? Then really start to pay attention to those thoughts, because once you bring them to the surface, you will start to catch yourself as you run on autopilot.

I suggest that you journal your thoughts and start to see them down on paper, in black and white. Once you do, you will catch yourself in those thought patterns. As you become more aware, when the negative thoughts show up, it's as simple as redirecting your brain. That new thought is now on autopilot. This is a practice, and it will not happen overnight, but it is worth taking the time to create it.

Your brain's job is efficiency, not hard work. Here's an action plan: One: understand it. Two: analyze it and ask, "Is it true?" Three: practice it. Notice every single day, day in and day out, what this consistent practice of being more mindful does for you.

You will find that it will become normal to think great thoughts like, *I don't think it's hard to get clients anymore.* What do you know now? I get clients. *I don't think that sales are hard to do any more.* And what do you know now? I'm excellent at sales, just like you start to see the G-Wagon or the big house in the neighborhood or the income potential that you never thought was possible. But again, what kills peoples' dreams most in life is impatience.

It doesn't happen instantly. It doesn't happen automatically. You have to do it for more than a couple of weeks. The how-to of this is really around practicing and doing the work and being disciplined and diligent.

You don't wake up every day feeling inspired, excited, and positive. But what you start to do is figure out what's going on in your head. Why don't you want the things that are going on? Are those thoughts about my day even true? And what do you need to think about instead to get what you want?

I suggest you practice it over and over and over again, and then hang out with those new friends who feel the same way that you feel. Now, all of a sudden, you're validated in your idea that getting clients is easy. Look at all these other people making all this money. And become the person who's making all of that money, too.

# 6

## YOU HAVE TO BELIEVE FIRST

If you're not sold on your success and worthiness, no one else will be. You have to know that the most important sale you'll ever make is the one to yourself.

Yes, I'm talking about worthiness. I think what happens is we start a business, start trying to get clients and make a difference with them, but then we get onto the entrepreneurial roller coaster. When we have a bad day, or don't get the client we wanted, we start tying our lack of worthiness with our business and then our lack of business success confirms our worthiness. That's the subject of this chapter. Let's dive in.

### The Most Important Sale You'll Ever Make

The best promise you will ever make is the one to yourself. Whether you are in sales or are an entrepreneur, believe first in yourself and then in the work that you do. You have to believe in the people that you serve, and in the value that you bring to the table. Otherwise, if you doubt any of those things, your business will struggle. If you think there is a better option, if you think there is a cheaper option, if you think there's too much competition, if you think that no one will ever pay you, if you think that you are not capable, or that you're going to screw stuff up, or you're not going to do good work for your clients, or any of the other myriad things that I have heard over the years, you will struggle to grow your business.

So even if the fire in your belly says, *go grow a business*, and you continue to show up in a lack of belief that you have the skill set, that you have the capability, and that the services that you offer are needed, you will always have trouble growing your business because you'll have trouble putting yourself out there.

This so often gets overlooked. We start a business because someone told us it should be easy to start a business, or we feel like starting a business because it's easier than going to work, or we took a sales role because it's commissioned and it's an opportunity to make more money, but we never really take the time to do the internal work of am *I sold on this position?*

We don't ask ourselves if we believe in what we're doing. I see this with new business owners. They start businesses because of whatever Facebook ad they saw, or whatever webinar they happened to watch. Once they start, they realize they're not at all that passionate about whatever it is they thought they wanted to do. And they wind up pivoting. Suddenly, their business takes off. And it's not because the business idea is better, it's because they are now sold on it.

There's a woman in my coaching program who came into the program as a general virtual assistant. That's what she thought she wanted to do. She wanted to do VA work so she could spend more time with her kids. She wanted to contribute to her family financially. About three or four months into the program, she was still struggling to sign a client.

She booked a call with me, and I asked her what was going on. She told me about her struggle to network and put herself out there. Once we really pulled her situation apart, we discovered it's because she has zero passion or emotional connection to being a virtual assistant. She said to me when I asked her about her VA business, "Yeah, it's fine. It's great, but it's not my jam. It's not my favorite thing to do."

I pivoted her into more creative work. She was still in the service provider arena, but doing more creative work, some writing and design stuff that allowed her to flex her creativity muscle, which she really enjoyed. All of a sudden, she was able to very quickly sign clients. And it wasn't because she couldn't have been an excellent virtual assistant. She just didn't believe in herself as a virtual assistant because it was not something she was passionate about. She just couldn't get that emotional connection that she needed to put herself out there.

If somebody had come to her and said, *hey, can you do the work for me?* I'm sure she could have done it, but to go out and actively sell the work? That was impossible for her because there was no emotional attachment. It showed up as fear. For you, it may show up as procrastination, or every week something comes up, like the kids get sick, or this and that interrupts your ability to sell.

When you lack passion, you find all these excuses to not work your business, but so often that is because you are not sold on what we're doing. You have to sell yourself on your service, on your ability, and on the idea that even in a saturated market, there is room for you because you're uniquely you.

## Market Saturation

When you consider market saturation, you must ask if you are sold on yourself. Why? Because what I am often told from perfectly capable people like you – life coaches, salespeople, virtual assistants, everyone – is that there's no room. The market is full of people who do what you do.

That is just another sign that you're not sold on yourself. You find evidence of the market being saturated. That is your proof. But let me tell you something, my friend, what you are looking at is not market saturation but your own lack of confidence about who you are and what you do.

I always use the example of multiple coffee shops on every corner. Or why there are four billion pizza joints in your hometown alone. There's a reason that there's four billion pizza joints. There's a reason why there are multiple restaurants, insurance agencies, and supermarkets in your town. *People need the products and services they sell.*

Let's look at competition as proof that there is money to be made. No competition means that you don't have a place – there may not be a market for what you offer – but if you are consistently viewing your market as saturated and your people as competition, you are showing yourself as someone who is not fully sold on the work that you do and your unique gifts to do that work.

When it comes to building confidence, I honestly think you become confident through practice. Confidence is a feeling. You can choose to feel confident, but oftentimes that feeling grows with practice. The more you want to do something, the better you get at it, the more confident you become. There's a lot of drama around "fake it 'til you make it." Some people totally believe in it.

I don't believe in the idea of walking around, making shit up. What I mean when I say "fake it 'til you make it" is that it is probably going to take you three times the amount of time to do this work because you're not used to doing it and you want to make sure that it's done exactly right.

I also believe in the whole "fake it 'til you make it" as a way to build your confidence. Keep putting yourself out there, do the thing you're afraid of, practice talking to people, and work with one or two clients for free by creating good boundaries around the free service so you build that confidence, build that muscle, and give yourself that proof and evidence that you can not only do the work, but you're skilled at it.

Even if you come across something that you don't know how to do, trust yourself to figure it out and find the resources that will teach you. Oftentimes building confidence is as simple as practice, but you can get trapped in this "chicken or the egg" problem: you want to have the confidence before you put yourself out there, but you've got to put yourself out there in order to build your confidence.

I think it's Tony Robbins who talks about "be, do, have." This means that you must be the person who does the thing to have what you want. I suggest that you must be a business owner who does the work in order to have success. You need to see yourself as the businessperson who can do the work that produces the results that you want to have.

Seriously, try this: take on the identity of the business owner or salesperson and then do the work for the business to be successful. What I see most often is my clients doing what they think it takes to have a successful business as proof to do the work, and that's backwards.

You're looking for "have, do, be," a kind of evidence to happen before actually doing the work. Here's the thing: you have to do the inner work to create the evidence.

## Feeling Confident in Your Pricing

There is another stigma out there about charging what you're worth. I believe that you can charge what you can confidently charge. You have all this drama around pricing, and you can go out and you can do research in any industry and you will find giant swings, right? I know you've seen this.

As an example, you can find a Facebook ad agency that charges $6,800 a month. And you will find a Facebook ad agency that charges $500 a month. That range of prices creates a lot of drama. You wonder, *where do I fit in here?*

Your thought process on pricing should be that you can start at a price that allows you to confidently look somebody in the eyes and say, "This costs X amount of dollars."

And then you raise your price from there. I think when you start at a high-ticket price, and your brain has not caught up with the idea that you are charging high ticket prices for what you do, you often stall your business growth. You go through this idea of *I should charge a high- ticket price because somebody who sells high ticket items told me I should.*

But because you can't feel (literally, in your body) the value of high-ticket sales, then you suck at selling high ticket sales. Whereas if you were to just start charging $500 a month and then $750 a month, and then $1000 a month, and finally build up to $2,500 a month, you would have gotten to $2500 with a greater number of sales much faster because you would be comfortable at each dollar increment along the way. You would have proof that you can sell at each price, and that builds confidence.

Let me be clear. It is not any easier to sell something inexpensive than it is something expensive. I have sold both. Your belief in it is what makes the difference. Over the course of almost two years, we took my Uncensored Sales Program from $99 a month to $750 a month. And our conversion rates never changed.

I had to build my belief that people would pay for it, that it was worth it, and that I could get those kinds of results. And that's what I did. We rolled out at $99 and then we went to $119 and then went to $149 and then we just continued to grow. The better the results we got our clients and the better we could talk to our ideal client avatar, the better results that we could show, the faster our clients were getting results, and the more that we were able to charge.

The more that I was able to confidently stand there and say, "This is 1000% worth that," the easier it was to raise the price over time.

Even in the beginning, I knew that I was undercharging. I knew that my program was worth much more than $99 a month, but I needed to build my confidence by selling it at the low price in order to get to the high-ticket price.

If I had tried to launch a $750 a month program from the start, I don't think the program would have ever become what it is because, at that time, I didn't have the confidence to say that I can help anyone create a six-figure business inside of twelve months because I had never done it before. But once I started seeing it happen, I started to better understand the types of clients who get these types of results.

We found that we worked really well in certain industries. We then started pivoting our marketing and our conversations, our pitches, and our sales conversations. Our conversion rates never dropped, nor the number of people in our launches as our price rose.

You can definitely undercharge, and if undercharging signs your first client and your second client and your third client, then do it. Do it for the short term. In other words, don't sign a long-term, twelve-month contract. This is meant to be a temporary situation. Take on a project that will take you six weeks, charge half of what you think you should charge, and then you can comfortably grow as you build your confidence. Ultimately you will make more money in the short term than if you try to charge what the industry says you should. Again, if you don't believe that your price is valid, if you don't believe that the work is worth it, nobody else is going to. You'll never get energetically aligned with your market and you won't sign a client at that price.

If you feel that paying a thousand dollars a month for social media management is outrageously high, you are going to struggle charging $1000 per month for your own program. You're not going to be able to sell social media management for $1000 a month.

Right now, as you're reading this, that dollar amount of $1000 may feel silly, but as your business continues to grow, your time becomes more valuable, and you're able to make more money, and $1000 a month might sound like a steal for social media management because of the amount of time that it frees you up.

If you're not energetically matched up with that dollar amount, you'll never be able to sell it. You could fake it and say it's a thousand dollars a month. But people can tell if you believe in the price, and if they sense your confidence, they will buy from you, thinking that your product or service is the best thing since sliced bread, that they got a fantastic deal, and they are happy about the purchase.

And they think that it is their duty to get this into your hands, get this into your life, get this into your business. Think of how that feels that versus the person who says, *it's a thousand dollars a month,* but you can feel them adding, *but you can get it across the street for half price.* You can hear it. You can feel it. I don't know how to explain it. I don't know how to teach it, but I just know that when you look at your price, if you feel like they could probably get it cheaper somewhere else, and it's probably better, you will always start underselling.

One of the things that I teach around pricing is that when you are pitching, explain why your offer is the exact right solution for your exact right problem. And you tell them that the best part is it's only going to cost them X amount of dollars. And you are not bullshitting as you say this. You genuinely feel that you can fix this problem for them.

After you tell them the price, you have to stop talking. You must shut up. It will be awkward. It will be uncomfortable. You will hate it. You will feel your heart start to race a bit. Your palms will start to sweat. You will literally have a physiological response to the discomfort.

The reason that this tactic or strategy works so well is because you are keeping your thoughts about the sale in your head, not your thoughts into their head. You have no idea how this person is processing this information that you have just shared with them. And if you start to talk or justify or explain or convince, you have lost the sale.

Selling is not about convincing. Selling is not about talking people into things. Selling is not about turning noes into yeses. Selling is about helping people make decisions. And as long as you're giving them your opinion on the pricing, which might sound like, *let me explain to you why I'm charging this much because I'm amazing, and I have all this experience,* they will be put off by the justification. For all you know, what they're thinking is, *wow, that's really cheap,* or *that's really expensive, but I need it anyway,* or *that's a great deal,* or *they're going to do all of that for only that dollar amount?*

But when your insecurity has you put your thoughts into the world, they hear it and start to think, *Gosh, maybe she's not worth it.* They're feeding off your energy and insecurity.

By staying quiet, you are giving them space so that whatever they say next is from their thoughts, their feelings, and emotions and not from yours. That is why the pause is so important. It feels very uncomfortable to do because, as humans, we don't like the dead air. We're afraid of the potential rejection. I recommend you take a deep breath and remain silent until they speak.

If you can physically change your body language, sit back and just be quiet. You can take care of your own mind. The silence is not going to be longer than a couple of seconds. It will feel like an eternity. Rarely is it longer than a couple of seconds because the other person is equally as uncomfortable as you are. They don't like the silence any more than you do.

But it is so important that it's their thoughts that come up next, whatever they have to say about the price. You want it to come from their brain because that's the only way you're going to sign them as clients. Because if you're giving them your thoughts, which are terrified or unsure, that's what you're going to get back. Nobody wants to buy a lack of confidence from you.

You don't want them thinking, *she doesn't even believe in her own ability to do this.*

## Believe the Work You Do Is Important

I would bet that you tend to think that, as a service provider and as the one who is selling, the person who is buying is more important than you. You think they have the power. You think they are the ones in control because they decide to give us their credit card or not, and the one who has the money is the one who controls the transaction.

Like it or not, sales is a power play. So often when you think the power is in the hands of your prospects, you start to say to yourself, "Oh, I'm just a virtual assistant." Or "I'm just a business coach," or "I'm just a salesperson." Whatever you do, you put the word "just" in front of it.

You downplay your work when you do this. And what you wind up doing is basically swapping out a job for entrepreneurship in which you continue to work for somebody else. But entrepreneurship isn't about working for somebody else. You're running a business. And the work that you do is important. Even if it is the work that people don't want to do.

Let me give you a great example. My client, Patricia, owns a cleaning company. When the 2020 shutdown happened, she was certain her business would tank because her clients had to send their employees home and the workspace would be unused.

Instead, she looked closely at the situation and turned her doubt into action. Patricia had commercial customers who remained open, and they needed someone to come in with the appropriate training and safety garb to clean and sanitize their spaces.

She added certifications. Patricia figured out what supplies she needed to be considered a "safe provider" and was able to secure additional clients because of her efforts.

She then pitched her certifications and her company's readiness at doing a great job during a crisis. Patricia told her existing and new clients, "I have a service that you need – a workplace environment where your employees know they are safe coming to work."

When you take something like cleaning, which most of us don't love doing, and adjust your mindset and consider that you offer an important service that people truly need, people will buy it at a premium.

I promise you, this company is not the cheapest company in town. But they have no problem signing clients because they have positioned themselves as an important part of their customers' business.

That is why you need to feel that the work you do is important. Even if the work that you do doesn't feel important in the grand scheme of things, it is. I'll give you another example. I work with a lot of bookkeepers, and some may say, "Oh, I'm just a bookkeeper." Notice how they use the word "just."

I reply to them with, "No, no, no, no, no. You help people better understand their money. You need to stop assuming that just because somebody can make money, that they know what the hell to do with it."

You must believe that as a bookkeeper, the work you do is important. It doesn't matter if the person you are serving has a super successful business and making money hand over fist. If they don't know how to balance their books, if they don't know what to do with their money, if they don't know the right way to set themselves up for success from a tax perspective, they're in trouble. You have got to see the importance of the work that you do. You are an important businessperson.

As an important businessperson, you have to show up in that way. I see this a lot, too, with my newer business owners, who wind up feeling like they're being interviewed by potential clients. My social media managers, my virtual assistants, and sometimes my bookkeepers, say they feel like they're interviewing for the job. No, you're not interviewing for a role. You are a business owner running a sales call. And while that may sound like semantics, it is an important mindset.

Remember this: You're not interviewing for a job. You are a business owner running a sales call. And I promise you, when you show up as a business owner running a sales call, you're going to be able to charge more. You are going to be well-respected and you're going to avoid taking jobs you don't want to because you will recognize when that person wants an employee, (but they're too cheap to pay for one, which is why they're hiring a contractor and not an employee to do the work).

You have got to believe that the work you do is important regardless of what that looks like. Remember, because somebody else is paying us money for our services, it does not mean that the person hiring has the power. The way I view it, I have the power because I have what the person who will hire me needs. Remember, whatever it is you sell, there is someone who needs it and will buy it. Showing up as the person who has the solution to the problem gives you the power.

Using me as an example, if you want to learn how to run a successful business, I can help you do that. You want to know how to sell confidently. I can help you do that. I'm an important businessperson here. It doesn't matter how much money I'm asking people for. And I promise you that through the course of my career, I have made millions of dollars for the companies that I worked for. My experience carries weight and I draw on it to be the one in the power seat.

## Throw People a Life Raft

I view my companies and what I can provide my clients as me throwing them a life raft. I solve massive problems in their business. I'm not taking their money. They are paying me because I have what they need.

Adjust your mindset to the difference between the person who charges $500 a month versus the person who charges $2,500 a month. It's the visible difference in what they think their services are worth. Your potential customer needs you in their business or in their life to get the results they want. That exchange of power is worth hundreds of thousands of dollars.

One of my clients experienced this mindset shift: she felt her potential client wanted to be in charge of the professional relationship and she knew this because the prospect treated my client like an employee who just supplied a service and brought little value beyond that. She was not considered a valued and trusted businessperson.

Let's be clear: anybody who's treating you like just a service provider is probably not an awesome client. I learned this when I worked in the corporate world and it's one of the big reasons why I wanted to become an entrepreneur. In corporate, we routinely took the money from those that wanted to treat us like we didn't know what we were doing while talking down to us and treating us like our work didn't matter.

You never have to accept business from a client who doesn't treat you or your team like a human because you're the service provider and they're the ones with the money. That dynamic and way of doing business was a huge motivator for me to start my own business and pick and choose the kind of clients that I want and love to work with.

Over the years, I've had so many people ask me who my ideal client is. I tell them that my ideal client is not just the one who can afford my service, but the one who can afford me and sees the value in the work that I do, who's a treat to work with and treats me like a respected human and business owner. That's the kind of client you want, too. I will not take just anyone's money, and you shouldn't, either.

When women start their business and take anybody as a client, that's a sign that they feel desperate. The mindset shift here is, even from the get-go, you can be selective. You don't have to work into being selective, or practice being selective. You can have the mindset of *I'm valuable* from the start. You can say, "What you're asking me to do is not something I do."

Keep seeing yourself throw a life raft out to those people who need your services. When you practice that, you'll always be in a position of power.

# 7

## TERRIBLE SALES ADVICE

### Sales Is a Numbers Game

We like to say that sales is a numbers game and we think we're being helpful when we say this. You win some sales, you lose some sales, and sometimes you lose more than you win. This is what happens. And to be honest, sales is a numbers game by volume, but when you approach it as just numbers, you can get stuck in a place that's not the best place for you to be.

Let me explain. When you are churning and burning through just outreach, you are working on numbers; specifically, the number of sales you can make.

You go about that by directing a message to four million people on Instagram or LinkedIn. Blindly. You set yourself up for failure when you blindly do this type of outreach. It's truly like throwing enough spaghetti at the wall to see what sticks. What sticks are the sales we make. Sure, you will have some success, but it's hard to duplicate because you've added all sorts of variables to the sauce – people who are and people who are definitely not your audience.

That is the churn-and-burn mentality where you burn through the leads without focusing on relationships, without focusing on reaching out to the right people, without focusing on being intentional with your activity.

Please don't misunderstand me: I do believe that sales is a numbers game because it requires a certain amount of volume to be successful. But you want to be intentional about who those people are.

Let's use Chet Holmes' statistic again that tells us only 3% of people at any given time are in the market for your services. So, if we're doing the math, and you want to sign three clients, you need to have 100 people in your ecosystem to make that happen.

It doesn't do any good to have a hundred people in your ecosystem if they're not the right people, even if they are looking for your services. Maybe they don't have the problem that you solve or are not in a position to buy because they may not be qualified in some capacity.

That's when the numbers game becomes an issue: when we're just using numbers for the sake of numbers. It doesn't feel good to have 100 people see that you sell to women when you have created an audience of a hundred men. You're never going to sign any clients. That's when it's not just about the numbers, it's also about the right people.

Now let's talk about your existing leads. How are you supporting them? How are you building relationships with them?

Again, there has to be a certain volume of activity to see success. You may have this idea of churn-and-burn and more outreach and more leads, which is easy to do in the social media world because you have access to so many people. It's easy for you to get super focused on new leads instead of thinking about the existing leads in your ecosystem. How are you supporting those people? How are you building relationships with those people?

You always need to bring new people in, but you also need to be moving people through your sales funnel all the time. Churn-and-burn does not allow you to do that because again, it's just more random activity instead of calculated, intentional activity focused on a specific outcome.

I see a lot of people fall victim to this mentality of mega-outreach, talking to tons of people and connecting to huge numbers of them every day. This leads to burnout and frustration, and negative replies to your direct messages, and then what happens? You stop selling altogether. It comes right back to how you are reaching out. That's how you fix this and still reach your numbers while being intentional.

First and foremost, it's about understanding who your ideal client is or who your ideal client might be. For instance, if you are a bookkeeper, then your ideal client must be a business that is making money. If you are a life coach for moms, your ideal client must be moms. If you are a mindset coach that works with six-figure entrepreneurs, then you want to make sure that's who ends up in your ecosystem.

Start by connecting to the right people on social media: Facebook, LinkedIn, Instagram, take your pick. But you have to concentrate on the right criteria for your ideal client. To qualify them, first look at who they are, what they do, and what they believe in.

You can tell the difference between a successful business and a business that is struggling based on their online presence. In fact, you might see some businesses that look successful, but aren't, but you're rarely going to find a business that is truly successful that doesn't also look successful online.

Check their website, their social media pages, podcasts, YouTube, and all the online spaces where business owners show up. It's usually pretty clear whether this person is making money or not.

That's your first order of business – figuring out who is a great fit by finding them online, assessing what they do and how they present themselves, and deciding are they a great fit for what you offer? Does this person fit the criteria of your ideal client? Yes or no? You can do that without ever having a conversation.

Let's say you're a life coach that works with moms. What do the moms you see online look like? If she's sharing pictures of her kids and family is a huge focus for her, then great. She's someone to add to your ecosystem. And you can do this from the comfort of your own home. This is why I love, encourage, and teach social selling.

Why is social media such a blessing? It's such an improvement over the way I grew up selling. We had to pull the door and shake the hand and talk to the people and actually drive by the business to determine if they were successful. I would even look to see if there were cars in the parking lot. That's how old school my sales experience is.

But today, social selling is the way to go. Start by looking at people's online profiles and then build a relationship.

I find the fastest way to qualify and get into conversation with someone is to make it about them and to start engaging with their social media content. The best way to get engagement is to get engagement, right? It's hard to ignore somebody who's all up in your stuff and liking, commenting, and responding to your stories in order to interact with you. What you first want to do is determine if this person fits the criteria from what you can tell, and then you want to get into a conversation, and there's a million different ways to do that. But ultimately, you're looking to see if this person fits those criteria.

Have conversations and figure out if this person has the problem that you solve or if they fit the criteria of the problem that you solve, in which case you would make an invitation to a sale.

I get hit a lot by people who are trying to sell me things. And if they just looked at my social media, they would not have pitched me through direct messaging. It's amazing to me that they do it. That's what I mean by churn-and-burn where they're thinking, *If I just direct message enough people, then eventually my person will raise their hand.*

But imagine what would happen if you only message people who actually fit the criteria of your ideal client.

You know, I remember somebody invited me to a presentation on how to have your first $5k month, and we were already at $50k months. You can't tell that by just looking at me, but if you saw how I show up online, and researched what I do online, you would see my large Facebook group, my podcast, that I have a group program and I've coached hundreds of women. That information alone would tell you to not pitch me how to make $5k per month.

That's the difference between qualifying people you're reaching out to, and the churn-and-burn mentality. Because, again, I do love outreach. It's part of what we teach in Social Sellers Academy. Outreach is how I built my career.

I think the churn-and-burn mentality comes from people

getting anxious about cold outreach. They think they need to jump into people's direct messages to pitch them stuff. And I don't know anything about them. I say outreach is about building a relationship with somebody new, based on a common ground that you can find on social media.

## Being in It for the Money

There is amazing money to be had in sales, but if all you're after is the money, you'll get bored as soon as you become successful. There's nothing wrong with being money motivated. I am money motivated. I love money. I love to talk about money. I love having money. I love spending money. I love investing money. I'm not saying that money is a bad thing. But if all the work you're doing is for the money, you'll burn out until you add an emotional reason for doing what you're doing. This is true if you're a sales rep or if you're an entrepreneur.

Let me give you a sales rep example. One of the sales reps on my team is relatively money motivated. When we were setting her goals for the year and I did the math on the amount of commission she could make, it was about $175,000.

That's a lot of money. There will come a point when you don't need more money. You have all the things that you want: a house, a car, the ability to travel, give to charities, whatever your jam is. But if it's just about having enough money, once you have enough money, what drives you?

What we wound up doing with my employee was brainstorm what the money could do for her. She wanted to update the hardwood floors in her mom's house. She wanted to travel, take a two-week vacation. That felt much more in line with why she wants to earn huge sums of money. Instead of working for the money and a big bank account, she's working for the vacation. She's working for this opportunity to get floors for her mom or working on an opportunity to buy a bigger house than she thought she could buy. I think her planning and goal setting is useful because what does the money mean unless you plan to use it in useful and fun ways?

Also ask yourself what value does it bring to your life? We know what the statistics are for people who win the lottery. They wind up worse off than they were when they won it.

We know the reason for that is because there's not a plan for that money. There's not a vision for that money. They don't wear the identity of somebody who has money and then they wind up losing it all. When you think about money, you have to become that person that makes whatever that dollar amount is for you – the travel, the bigger house, whatever it may be. I think it's really important from a sales rep's perspective, but also for the entrepreneur who is making sales. You will have to deal with this as your success soars.

## Focus on the Sale Instead of the Relationship

Most entrepreneurs that I talk to daily are mission driven. But I have found people burn themselves out in the business because they were after money instead of doing work. Here's the deal: growing a business is hard work. A lot of people won't tell you, *oh, hustle culture is bad.* But you know, while building a business is hard work, there is no reason for you to work that hard. If you're doing work that you don't enjoy, that doesn't light you up, or you're just doing the work for money, go find a job. That'll probably pay you more money and you won't have all the stress, pressure, and responsibility that goes into being an entrepreneur.

Money can be part of the driving factor. I readily admit that I'm very money-motivated, but making money must be about your why and your mission. Where are you going with your business? What's important to you? What are you going to do with that money? Start by making plans and ideas for your money. It will really help. My husband and I both grew up as athletes. We both feel strongly that athletics are a fantastic way to learn life skills and stand out. One of the things that we want to do is partner with, or develop if it doesn't exist, a sports organization in inner city areas where kids might not get to play elite sports because cost is a barrier to entry.

Whether it's a program you want to offer, or you want to partner with someone who allows kids to play elite sports despite their family's financial situation, or you want to be the ticket to end generational poverty and help kids get into college, remember that those are dreams worth having.

When I think about you making a lot of money, I always want to ask, "What are you going to do with that much money?" What does that much money even look like mentally? I'm able to really drill down to imagining change – that a kid's life improves because they get to play sports, they get to travel, and they get to experience things they never would have before. How much better does that set them up for success, even if they don't go on to be collegiate or professional athletes? Being part of a team in their teenage years can make a huge difference to them.

As you can see, that's one of the things I'm especially passionate about.

## The Identity of Money

This ties into a mindset around money and having a certain perspective about money instead of just seeing money as the be-all-end-all. It's about showing up as the person who's going to make the money, and not as a reflection of your emotional drive.

Let's go back to the lottery winner example. Here is a person who has never identified as a wealthy person. If that's their reality, then once they are wealthy, they often lose their money.

This can happen to us as entrepreneurs and salespeople, right? You have to start wearing a wealthy identity and start thinking that wealth is yours to have. You can even start saying, "I have the ability to create wealth for myself."

When you think about money and just being in business for the money, you may start to worry about being a bad person. This is a problem because you have to show up as the person who is available and open to making a lot of money.

## Not Clients. Relationships.

This goes back to the numbers game idea. One of the things that I have probably said the most in my coaching career is that you need to stop looking for clients and you need to start building relationships. The reason that you "can't find clients" is because you are looking at every single person as a client, potential client, or potential paycheck instead of viewing the person as a relationship.

You have probably experienced sales tactics in which the person doesn't let you off the phone without collecting a payment or doesn't give you the price until you agree to talk to the rep on the phone. All these strategies are about tricking or manipulating you into buying.

And that's why sales has such a bad reputation – because you think it's all about manipulation to get someone's money instead of being focused on building relationships. And through that relationship, you're able to solve a problem and sell, which is where the magic happens.

This is when sales feels good – when you're showing up compassionately. You're showing up with service in mind. You're showing up with heart. You're showing up to make an impact in a positive way.

I know, especially if you're new to business or you're new to sales, that if you are thinking about goals to hit, your focus changes to selling for the sake of meeting those goals and you're not staying focused on building relationships. You then start resisting sales and it becomes harder to close business because each person in your inbox, each person you interact with on social media, is about a sale and not about the person. When you detach from the need to sell something and focus on connecting with people, you will sell more.

I know that sounds like an airy-fairy idea. But I promise you – through those connections, you will establish relationships that will be rich with possibilities. Relationships equals clients. Every single person that you meet is a potential client, a potential referral partner, a potential collaboration partner, and a potential new friend.

The person who helped me with the writing of this book was a woman who went through my coaching program, worked with us for twelve months in my Uncensored Sales program, and has a kickass business. When I went looking for somebody to help me write a book, I obviously went looking in my network. Someone said, "Why don't you talk to Katie?" I didn't even realize that was a service that she offered, but because I already knew her, liked her, trusted her, and we already had a relationship, it was a very easy decision for me to hire her.

I had an introduction from someone else in my mastermind group, but I chose the person that I had a relationship with. That's how people do business.

Getting to know people and what they do makes life so much easier. Whether you're trying to sell something, or you need to buy something, your network is a resource of potential ongoing and repeat sales. If I had just focused on selling my services to Katie and never getting to know her, I would have never had an opportunity to work with her.

Sometimes you don't realize that the conversations you have with people are leading to a sale. The people aren't talking about it, but you're getting to know them. Then they may tell you they're interested in your services. I admit that I've had this happen a couple of times. The conversations and new relationships led to sales and opportunities.

Today's buyer has too much information. They have too many choices for sales to ever be about convincing or forcing them to do business with us. I consider this a male mentality of going out and meeting as many people as possible, asking the exact right questions to get the exact right answers, and then force and convince you to buy. It starts with a forceful pitch, too. If you are at all curious, then you experience a negative form of "encouragement" to get you to say yes.

Sure, there will be some people who say yes, and give the salesperson money because they are incapable of saying no. My husband Kevin is one of them. He would hand over his money just to shut the salesman up. There is nothing between Kevin and the salesman but pushy selling. Nothing else.

When you talk about not being focused on the numbers and not being focused on the money and not being focused on just closing the business but instead being focused on connecting with the right people while focusing on your inner why, you won't show up as the sales rep who pushes. Instead, you know why you're connected to what lights you up so you can focus on building relationships with people because you know the relationship can bring you opportunities.

Some of my very best friends are other business owners. They're women I've met who have bought stuff from me and I have bought stuff from them. I've referred them to a million different people and they're literally some of my closest friends.

This is when business is so much fun that all you want to do with your business is meet awesome people and help them flourish and prosper. That feels good to the core of who you are as a human being. I love being able to help other people because then it always comes back to me, as it will to you, too.

I mentioned it before: you need to become known before you're needed. What does that mean? As you increase your coffee chats, you will ultimately build a network with people who might not need whatever it is you do right now. But when they do, they already have a relationship with you. So instead of going to Google, Facebook, or any social media, they will come to you first.

You will hear people say they have a need for a social media manager. That's when you can say you had coffee with one last month who was brilliant and had fantastic ideas. Would you like an introduction?

That is an example of becoming known before you're needed.

I once had somebody tell me that they thought that coffee chats and networking were a waste of time because you wind up on the phone with random people. I say that's the point! You want to be on the phone with random people because you never know when you may need that random person. Or the random person is in the market for your services. This is when I say stop focusing on the sale and focus on relationships.

And they're like, "That's the point? Will that random person, who might not be in the market for my services now, eventually be in the market for my services?" You will only know when you focus on getting to know the business owner to see what their goals are. Again, stop focusing on the sale and focus instead on the relationship.

To the person who said they get all their business from referrals – this is how it works. You meet people and sell yourself before the person you meet needs your service. They may come back to buy from you or refer their own friends, family, and acquaintances.

Referrals all come out of building relationships. I want somebody to have my name in their mind before they ever go to Google or go to their followers on Facebook and ask for the kind of help I provide. Instead, I'd rather get work from someone who has a relationship with me already.

In turn, I want to be the person that somebody sends an email to and says, *hey, I'm looking for help with this. Can you connect me?* That's what I'm looking for when it comes to relationships. I have tons of people in my inbox asking for connections and recommendations because I've networked so much.

# 8

## YOU ARE IMPORTANT

### The Work that You Do Is Important

Let's start with the idea that the work you do is important. What often winds up happening to you as a service provider or a sales professional? You start feeling like you are at the mercy of the people who buy things from you. You wind up feeling like the person with the money, the person buying your products and services, has all the power, and you are just a service provider. You're just the business owner. You're just the salesperson that needs a sale from them.

What tanks more businesses and sales careers than anything else is thinking that the people who need what you sell have all the money and all the power. You start thinking thoughts like, *I have no power. I am bothering people. I'm an imposition, or an annoyance.*

I want to remind you what Mike Weinberg, a sales author,

says, "You are an important businessperson. The work that you do is important. You solve important problems for people."

So instead of believing that they hold all the power because they have the money and they get to make a buying decision, flip that idea on its head and know that you are the one with the power. You have the answer that can solve the problem. They don't have <u>power</u>; they have a <u>problem</u>.

Repeat your solution to yourself: I can help you make more money. I can help you lose weight. I can help make your life better. I can help improve your relationships. I can, whatever problem it is that you solve, help you. Make a mindset shift to the idea that the work you do is important in the world.

I know some of you are thinking, *hey Ryann, you know I'm a VA, right?*

Do not diminish your skills. As a VA, if you can give a business owner back ten hours a week in their business, and in those ten hours they are able to go on and create an additional seven figure income stream in their business, then guess what? You are not just a VA. You are essential.

And I bet that person would admit that you are an important part of their business. Are you the one driving the revenue? Maybe not, but you are the one creating the space for that person to drive revenue. Think about it that way because it's an important shift in your perspective.

Let's use a business to consumer example. You might be a health coach who knows of so many cheaper options to help people lose weight. They could go to Weight Watchers. They can get a gym membership. And your thoughts end up saying, *why would they pay me a thousand dollars a month for one-on-one coaching when there's all these cheap groups and less costly options?* The truth of the matter is A. They probably tried all those cheaper, lesser options with no results, and B. You give them customized support to lose weight.

You are the one with the power. They're the one feeling over-weight and uncomfortable and not wanting to go to the pool with their kids, or not wanting to go on a date with their spouse. They feel unhappy in their body. You are not bothering that person by reaching out to them. You are not bothering them by selling your services. You are helping them. You are making their life better.

Arguably, you might be one of the most important people in their life, because what if they're able to lose that weight and in losing that weight, they show up more confidently and they get a promotion at work, or they finally decide to leave that job, start a business, and go on to create a multimillion-dollar busi-ness because they feel good in their skin again?

Repeat after me: *The work you do is important.*

Remember Patricia? The woman in my coaching program who runs a successful cleaning company? I have literally worked with Patricia since I started my company. She could say she runs a cleaning business and Patricia knows that a lot of people call it an awful job. But she also knows that's not true. She looks at her cleaning company as the reason why families have their weekends back. Patricia owns a company that helps families create more memories.

If you own a cleaning company, your work is important because now your clients get to spend the weekend at the park with their kids while your team is cleaning their house.

If you're struggling to understand what is important about your work, a great idea is to sit down with a piece of paper and brainstorm all the ways that somebody's life or business is improved by working with you. Now, start showing up that way. Instead of being just the person who cleans houses, or offers virtual assistant services, show up as the person who transforms someone's life.

You are not just a coach, or a bookkeeper, or an operations consultant. No, no, no, no, no, no. Even if you transform people's lives in the simplest ways, your work is important. You solve problems. You give people back their lives. You give people back additional income streams. You give people back their memories.

Let's talk about the word "just." We like to use the word just to shrink into what we do. And I really hate that word. It diminishes how important the work is that we do. Drop the use of that word today and remember, you are important.

## Show Up as a Professional

With that said, because the work that you do is important and because you solve really big problems for people, you need to show up as a professional. An example that I've used before is the physician. Doctors go to school forever! (I watch a lot of *Grey's Anatomy*, so I should know!)

But seriously, they are professionals, they show up professionally, and they do tons of continuing education. They show up as doctors and offer their medical expertise.

Entrepreneurs have a tendency, because maybe your business isn't making a lot of money yet, or because it's just a side hustle while you're raising kids or you consider it just this thing that you do, that you don't always show up looking and acting like a professional. But it's true that to be successful, to make the money you want, you must start acting like a pro.

Right now, everyone's on Zoom. How are you showing up?

This isn't a section about hair and makeup. If you don't want to wear makeup, that's fine, but using small things like a decent mic and a ring light makes the difference in how you show up. I know many, many women are growing businesses around families and there are kids at home and all that other stuff, but does the person that you're talking to feel important? Do they feel valued? Do they feel like you're paying attention, or do they feel like you're distracted?

You may think it's no big deal to be in yoga pants and a sweatshirt, but you're making an impression on someone, whether it's intentional or not. You're making an impression on someone, in some way, shape, or form. The work that you do is important regardless of what that looks like, and you want to show up professionally and prepared because that gets you clients and customers.

Another example of this: Don't ever get on a coffee chat without doing a Google search of the person you're meeting. Don't ask questions that you could find the answer to online. I call them lazy questions. I refuse to answer questions about what I do when those kinds of emails show up in my inbox. The person behind that email just lost their credibility. If she bothered to take 90 seconds to look at my social media profile and figure out what I do, then the questions would be different, smart, and show me they are credible. Then I may respond.

That's what I mean by showing up professionally. The work that you do is important, but you have got to treat it like it is important. You've got to put yourself in a position to leave a lasting impression, to build a relationship. You want to create the situation where you're known before you're needed.

If you want those referrals to start coming in, you have to show up like you care, like you're prepared. Like, *hey, you know, I checked you out on LinkedIn.* Or, *I checked you out on Facebook,* or *I joined your Facebook group* or *listened to your podcast.* There are many different ways that you can learn about someone that will take you zero time but allow you to create a great connection.

To use the physician example again: doctors study all the time. They're constantly looking for new and better ways to do things. They maintain a high level of professionalism by being trained and skilled at what they do. And they show you how professional they are by being able to answer your medical questions.

If you want to be viewed as important, if you want to be a sought-after professional, if you want to hit your income goals, you have to show up as a professional. That includes being trained and knowing answers. And be willing to find them if you don't know the answer.

My business coach and business partner, Kelly Roach, says we need to train for business just like athletes train for sports. She literally will tell you she likes to work with business athletes. Why? Because, as a professional athlete, you train, you study, you do the work, and you show up on the days that you don't want to practice. You practice anyway, over and over again. Yes, the work that you do is important, but you need to treat it like it's important. You need to treat it like it is a profession. It's your career. It's your legacy. It's your livelihood.

I may be perceived as old school, but it really does matter how people show up with me online. When I'm doing coffee chats and the person looks like they dragged themselves out of bed, I am skeptical of them and their abilities. I know everybody has a rough day and I can overlook a lot of things, but to me, that's a huge red flag.

One of the women in my Sales Accelerator program was

scheduling coffee chats and talked about how brutal they had been. She said no one Googled her or visited her website. They didn't know anything about her. She knows she's speaking to moms and they're busy – we all are – but come to the chat prepared. Otherwise, you waste valuable time-sharing information that both of you should know at the start of the call. Plus, knowing who you are speaking to raises the level of conversation that you have, and frankly, is a really polite thing to do!

I work with other moms and sometimes they show up in yoga pants. My take is this: if you don't care that somebody doesn't want to work with you because you're in yoga pants, then game on sister, wear the yoga pants. If that judgment is not important to you in any way, and you only want to work with people that are 100% okay with your style choices, and your kids are around all the time, that's okay. But if that's not what you want and that's not the impression you want to give, then treat your business like a professional. Wear professional clothes and have someone watch your children during your calls.

One of the biggest things, and this ties into our first point, is this: your work is important, and sales is all about follow-up. Remember the Chet Holmes statistic that 3% of your potential clients are in the market for your product and services at any given time? That means 97% of them are not. That means we also must follow up with the 97% because at some point, they will need your services. How do we do that? We build relationships. Sometimes this leads to drama about the follow up. You don't want to appear pushy. You don't want to appear salesy.

The way that I reframe this is to say that you are talking to consenting adults on social media, and you have all agreed to be there. They know who you are and are okay with being on social media with you. When contacted, they also have the power to say no thank you should you contact them.

Now, I'm not saying it's okay to be spammy or pushy, but so often we reach out and chat with people and they never get back to us. That is your invitation to follow up. Of course, I have been told by clients, "I did follow up once, but I never heard back."

I tell them to follow up again, and the next excuse I hear is, "I don't want to bother them." You are not bothering them if you have provided them with a service or product they truly need. They want to know that you are willing and available to help them. So, help them by following up.

## Are You Being Pushy or Are They Being Rude?

Not replying and not responding to your direct messages or emails is due to one of two things: people are busy. There are so many messages coming at people all the time and they may or may not remember to circle back with you. They have a lot of things on their plate. Second, they don't want what you have to offer.

My thoughts about this? If I've had a conversation with you and you expressed interest in what I do, I am following up to help you solve a problem. That's not being pushy; it's being persistent. There's a big difference between the two. Being pushy is sending direct messages every day asking for the sale, or emailing with an edge to your voice and inquiring as to why you haven't followed up.

Being persistent is asking politely, "How can I help you? When would you like to start? Has anything changed since we last spoke that I can help you with?" You are more likely to respond to that and say, "Now's not the right time," or "I'm just not interested," or "I'd love it if you circled back to me in 90 days."

When you're thinking *I don't want to be pushy*, remember that they are not worried about being rude to you, and some people will be rude. If that's the case, why are you worried about being pushy when you're just asking them for a reply? That's not being pushy or being rude. You are being helpful.

When you don't reply to my pitch, I assume that you're too busy, swamped with work, or overwhelmed. My clients will often tell me that they assumed the potential clients they talked to changed their mind. One of my clients did just that, except I surprised her by becoming her first big contract, her first big retainer client. She did all the things she needed to close the sale, sent the contract, which I signed, and then the invoice, which got paid.

In the instance where you've had a conversation with someone and they haven't expressed an interest in committing to work with you, it is your job, no, your duty to follow up. It is my obligation to be persistent in helping you get the result that you said that you wanted. I could imagine you saying, "I can't afford it," or "I'm not ready now," or "It's not the right time." Or maybe you were excited about the project at first, but something shifted in your thinking and you don't want to work with me after all.

Yet another client followed up three times with a prospect and never got a response back. She felt defeated and done. She even said, "I'm done here." Then she found out that someone in the prospect's family had been diagnosed with cancer. On the fourth follow up, her prospect told her not only what was going on, but then said, "I still want to do this. I just need two more weeks."

All this time, my client was thinking the woman didn't want to work with her, decided that her pricing was too high, that she's not any good, and that none of this was going to work. That extended to nobody was ever going to hire her and she was never going to find the secret sauce of success.

I look at follow up as normal and never as pushy, and people who don't reply are being rude. Or maybe they are dealing with some sort of life experience, but I will keep following up until they say yes or they say no.

Stand your ground as an important businessperson who solves an important problem for people and gets them results. When you look at people as both valuable and important, you're going to be persistent. I can't tell you the number of times over my corporate career people told me, "Hey, we're doing business with you because of your persistence."

When you view the person on the other side of the direct message, or the other side of the conversation, as the one with all the power, you're just over here waiting for somebody to be willing to pay you. Instead, know that what you do is important, and the results that you get for your people are amazing, and the impact that you make is huge. Decide to adopt a relentless pursuit for helping people. You want to give them what they need and in turn, you build your business. Pursue them with persistence.

I have had many people not only respond to my follow ups but thank me for following up. You know what they say – the fortune is in the follow-up.

## 9

# THE WORDS YOU USE MATTER

## How You Talk to Yourself

The words you use matter. This concept ties in directly to the idea of being and seeing yourself as an important businessperson. One of the biggest opportunities I see for women in sales and business when it comes to improvement is their use of passive language. I often hear them ask, "What are your thoughts on this? Maybe we could do this. Let me know what you're comfortable doing."

The words chosen, the way they are asked or stated, and the fact that you think it's okay to say this is a huge red flag with regard to how you think of yourself. These words make women lose their credibility. Why? It sounds like you don't know what the hell you are doing. You are asking for permission and waiting for approval from someone else.

As an important businessperson who solves important problems for people, you need to control the conversation. You cannot control the conversation when you're asking for permission to run the conversation. You don't have to be aggressive in your language, but using powerful words helps raise your credibility and that's a much better way to present yourself.

Here are some examples I see in my inbox daily: *I'm sorry to bother you.* Or, *Hey, no big deal. If this is not a fit for you, but if it is, what are your thoughts on this?* Or *I'd love to get your opinion on this.*

You think these are ways of avoiding being aggressive, but what's actually happening is you're losing your credibility by putting yourself in the passenger seat of your business building journey. When you talk or write like this, you are waiting for other people to agree or give you the power or say it's okay. How you show up in a sales conversation, how you control your sales conversations, and how you wear the hat of a trusted advisor very often shows up in the language that you use.

Again, I'm not saying you need to be aggressive. I'm not saying you have to bulldoze people. And I'm not saying that you have to talk over people or interrupt them. This is about showing up confidently and professionally. When you truly believe that what you do makes a giant impact in the world and that you can help people, you need to use language that communicates that.

## How You Talk to Prospects

Another pattern goes like this: you tend to use a whole lot of words when five or six would do. You do that as justification. Before you start a conversation, you find yourself thinking, *I'm justifying why I'm reaching out to you. I'm justifying why I'm following up with you. I'm justifying why I'm asking this question.*

THE 100K SALES METHOD

Just ask the question and be done. Adding all those words is projecting your own insecurity and fear into the sales conversation.

Nobody wants to buy from somebody who is insecure. Nobody wants to buy from somebody that sounds like they don't know what the hell they're talking about. Admit it. You DO know what you're talking about. I know that you know what you're talking about, but the language that you're using makes it sound like you are asking for permission.

As long as you continue asking for permission, you might sign some clients, some deals, but you are never going to hit the goals that you want to hit because true professionals – business-people and salespeople – use direct language to communicate. I don't mean aggressive language, just direct language. Say what you mean and mean what you say kind of language. Often my clients will ask me when they are preparing to ask for the sale, "How do I say this?" And I reply, "Just like that. Just ask the question."

If you have a question, ask the question. One of my favorites is people who dance around the budget question. I find out if the prospect has any money. I just ask, "Hey, do you know what you have earmarked to accomplish this project?" That's how you have the budget conversation. You don't dance around it. You don't try to hypothesize. How much would you invest? Are you willing to invest?

Come to a place where you're having a sales conversation. Your prospect has a problem. You have a solution. You now need to know what they can pay for your solution.

*What is your budget?*

*What do you have earmarked to solve this problem?*

You must be direct because when you dance around that

question, you create problems like A) You aren't communicating on the same page, and B) You are setting yourselves up for disappointment because you may think this person has the budget, but they don't. Because you didn't ask any questions about it, you end up with a problem.

You end up in a place where you're backpedaling in your conversations, and it's not serving you in any way, shape, or form. Want to know how I would get a second meeting with this person? I'd ask for a second meeting. How do you tell them you can help them? You tell them you can help them. Be direct.

There has been so much misinformation perpetuated in the business space. Many people are convinced sales is about fancy words and slight of tongue when really, sales is about meaning what you say and saying what you mean. End of story. That's how you earn respect. That's how you become a trusted advisor. That's how you demand a premium for your services. That's how you conduct business as a professional businessperson. How many times have you had a conversation with someone and thought, *I have no idea what they just said because they used 400 words when they could have used 20*. Don't be that person.

Here's another sales gem: being direct also moves the sales process forward. In fact, you know that it moves the sales process along because you broach and resolve the topics like budget that often makes the prospect uncomfortable, especially if you're the salesperson. It gets it all out in the open, and the fact that you don't bury it under bunches of words helps to move it along. People are relieved. I've even seen relief on people's faces, as though they are thinking, *Thank God that's over. Let's keep going.*

When you are uncomfortable, it's because you think there is something wrong with charging for your services. That comes back to you believing that you've charged too much. People will see value in the conversation because they don't understand something, but if you are doubtful and insecure, you are communicating, *I don't believe in what I do.* And they won't believe you can help them.

Sales is the transfer of inspiration. It motivates people into action. When you use passive, weak language, it doesn't inspire anyone into action. You're apologizing for your existence. You're apologizing for charging what you do. Nobody wants to do business with the person who apologizes.

While you think that you are doing yourself or that person a favor, or you're making the conversation more enjoyable, or you're not being pushy, you are actually showing up as weak. You may think that you are demonstrating these thoughts, *I want my relationships with clients to be a collaboration. I want to work with dream clients.* You think that the only way to do that is to give up a layer of power and your powerlessness shows up in your language.

It's the exact opposite when you show up in your power and think, *I can confidently solve this problem for you. I am confident in my pricing. I am confident in the results that I can get for you.*

That's how you attract dream clients. That's how you have productive, painless sales conversation. That's how you make money.

My advice is to stop apologizing for being good at what you do. Stop apologizing for being direct. Stop apologizing for expecting people to hold up their end of the bargain. When you talk about someone who doesn't respond to you, stop apologizing for that person. Let them go and move on.

It'll be a little uncomfortable at first to change your language from passive to confident. Once you start speaking in an active voice, you'll be able to very quickly figure out who your people are and who they are not. The reason you use passive language is because you don't want to find out it's a no. When I sell, I want to know you're a no as quickly as possible so I can stop wasting my time and my brain space. Perhaps you've done this where you don't ask for the sale because then your prospect can't tell you no. Except there's nothing wrong with a no. It's a complete and truthful answer.

Dodging a rejection can start to look like you're creating a pool of leads or prospects who might or maybe someday, if you're lucky, trip and fall and actually pay your invoice. You were nice in the process. There's some thinking that, *If I'm nice, they'll come around.* You can be direct and be nice. Those two things are not mutually exclusive.

Think about this: **the kindest thing that you could do in the sales process is to be direct and be honest.** Since sales has such a bad reputation of shadiness, lying, misinformation, and manipulation, the kindest thing that you could do in the sales process is communicate directly and clearly in as few words as possible. Speaking that way takes all the sales sliminess out. You won't be told that you're trying to manipulate someone when you're using as few words as possible to explain the situation. You can't feel like you're trying to trick them when you ask a direct question like, "Do you have a budget for this?" You're not trying to trick them into telling you that they have more money when you're asking a direct question about their budget!

To get rid of the stigma around sales, you need to use more direct language. Not the language you see in the movies that's fast-talking and tricks you into saying yes multiple times. That's not what you're doing here. You're building relationships. You're

THE 100K SALES METHOD

solving problems. You're being direct and respectful and owning your power through the process.

There's nothing worse than a sales conversation that goes like this: "Well, I might maybe be able to, sort of, kind of do this for you." Wouldn't you rather buy services from the person who says, "Hey, no problem. I got this. What's your budget? What's your timeline for getting it fixed?"

## What to Do About All the Negative Self-Talk

How do you talk to yourself so that you don't come off as a weenie in a sales conversation? You know it covers both mindset and sales. Again, when you talk to a prospect, the words you use matter. I would argue that they almost matter more than the way that you talk to yourself. Here's some language I suggest you stop using:

- *I hope this is a good sales call.*
- *I hope they pay the invoice.*
- *I hope they sign up.*
- *I hope they're a good lead.*
- *I hope they're interested in what I do.*

You keep hoping they might be interested. They might sign up. They might show up for your conversion event. They might, they might, they might. There's nothing wrong with saying that because you genuinely do hope for it.

If you are telling yourself, *I have to be likable. I have to be agreeable,* understand that's only the story in your head. I often coach women on the ways they talk to themselves leading up to the sales call, along with how to set themselves up for success.

When you walk into a sales call, I want you to stop thinking, *I hope they were a good lead that ends up a sale. I hope they are a good fit. I hope they have the money. I hope that they're interested.*

Your negative self-talk gives away your power, right? You've already talked about how much power is in your words and what happens when you give it away.

Reminder: you want your self-talk before the sales call to sound like, *I am super pumped to talk to this person. They are the perfect lead. I know they're going to see so much value in what I do. I love everything that I can find about them. I am so pumped to have this conversation.*

The person that shows up in that conversation is very different from the person that shows up in the *Gosh, I hope that, maybe, they sorta kinda want to buy.*

I know this sounds a little woo, but the conversation that you have with yourself every single time you show up on a sales call, every single time you show up on a networking call, every single time you send an email, every single time you send a direct message, every time that you reach out to somebody, is going to change how you show up in your business.

You can't be interesting or interested if you are second guessing every single move that you make and you are doubting yourself and your language while talking down to yourself. You know you do it all the time, but it's time to stop the thoughts of *Oh, I totally messed up. I did it wrong. I totally ruined that sales conversation. I totally missed the opportunity.*

I hear this from women all the time. While it might be possible that you totally flubbed the conversation, beating yourself up over it is not going to change that fact. What it will do is make it more likely that you flub the next conversation and the next conversation and the one after that.

The better conversation that you have with yourself after you flub is, *So, yeah, that was not my best performance, but you know what? I'm practicing. I learn from every single opportunity. Now I know next time that I need to do this, this, and this. Next time I'm going to ask this question.*

The words you use to describe yourself and your business, even small things, are what make you who you are. *I'm trying to get my virtual assistant business off the ground.* That feels true. However, *I'm trying to make this work* may be true, but that language sets you up for a place where you can't lift yourself to success.

Instead try, *I'm willing to do whatever it takes to get my virtual assistant business off the ground.* That even sounds better. It changes the way you feel and when you feel better, you show up differently.

The words that you use, how you talk, how you have to become like your own biggest hype girl, are important. You must hype yourself up. If it helps, get a piece of paper, and give yourself five minutes before a sales conversation to write down all the reasons why it's going to be a fantastic conversation.

It doesn't matter if they buy or not. You're going to show up as the best version of yourself. The way that you have that conversation, the language, the internal dialogue about your business, about your work, about your ability, about your value, all of that is impacting how you show up.

Show up and say, *I'm going to follow the exact blueprint I know that I need to follow. I'm going to solve people's problems.* Just say that to yourself out loud. *I'm good at what I do. People see a ton of value in having conversations with me, whether or not they buy, it's going to be a fantastic conversation.* Say that out loud and see how you feel.

Fake it till you make it will help you change the way you feel. Don't pretend to be someone you're not. Tell that mean, nasty voice in the back of your head that tells you *Who the hell am I to be starting a business? Who am I to be asking people for that amount of money? Who am I to be doing this?* to sit down and shut up. Sometimes the only way that you can do that is to spend five minutes writing down all the reasons why you're amazing at what you do. The way that you talk to yourself is arguably more important than the way that you talk to your prospect.

I promise you, if your inner dialogue is good, you wouldn't show up apologetically, right? You wouldn't use passive language. You would show up with confidence. You would show up excited. You would show up standing in your power. The passive language you use for your prospects comes from the chatter in your brains, and that chatter can be changed. The old, passive chatter comes from self-doubt. It comes from second guessing. It comes from whatever mean girl is still back there telling you you're not good enough. Change it.

I have clients that will come to me, and they say, "Well, I'm really hoping that we do this, this and this by the end of the month." I suggest to them that they reframe what they just said to something like, "I am so excited to sign 10 new clients." This mantra feels very different, and much better.

Come from a place of opportunity, excitement, and possibility as well as abundance. There are a million books on sales and business, and there are so many resources out there. I run paid programs teaching people how to do this, but I promise you that there are more than enough free resources out there for anybody to be wildly successful.

That's what the inner dialogue does for you. I'll give you an example. I was in Nashville, on vacation with my family, and I had to take an Uber back to my hotel. I had just had lunch with a colleague and my family had gone home. As I was heading back to my hotel, I chatted with the Uber driver.

He told me that Nashville is growing like crazy and houses that used to be $150,000 are now well over $400,000 and how this is going to price the middle class out of ever being able to afford a home. He was of the opinion that building all these apartment buildings that were renting for well over $2,000 a month... who could possibly afford that?

He continued, "You've got to be making so much money to be able to spend that amount of money on rent every month. You know, people are never going to be able to buy houses and there's going to be a housing market crash."

It was all doom and gloom with this dude. I know all about gloom and doom. Overcoming that kind of thinking is the mindset work that I've done over the years. I'm not saying that my thinking turned around overnight, but it's at a point where, while I listened to this guy, instead of seeing doom, all I saw was opportunity.

My mindset said they are beautiful apartments that people are going to put up some significant cash, which means they're going to be well taken care of. They're going to be cool places to live because they're not charging $400 a month. They're renting for $2000. It's going to get a better quality of renter. It's going to create a better community.

He could have said, "Imagine how much money is going to come to Nashville because of what's happening to the city. How many more concerts are we going to get? How many of our sporting events are going to be filled because people love Nashville? How many new companies are going to build their headquarters here because it's a really cool place to live?"

The only difference between his thoughts and mine was our perspectives. The circumstances were the same. A housing crisis going through the roof, brand new apartments with high-end rents, lots of traffic, lots of updating of highways. This guy's inner dialogue was, *Man, this is terrible.* And I was over here thinking, *Hell yeah for opportunity in Nashville, and thank goodness for inner conversations where we pick the words to use, know that words matter, and how specifically it's important to all of us how we talk to ourselves.*

This guy felt just like a victim. Everything was good, but his thoughts were settled on victimhood. The thing is, this poor guy in Nashville didn't know any different. He didn't know how to switch his thinking from suffering to success. That was a huge difference between us.

So, now you're here reading this book. Hopefully, you're listening to your own thoughts: the words that you use, the way that you describe your situation. Here's a different Uber story that a friend of mine told me.

She was attending a conference in Boston and after her day at the conference, called Uber to take her back to her Airbnb.

She asked her driver why he drove for Uber. He was happy to say that he had a successful import company, but it didn't make enough for him to pay for his daughter's tuition to Harvard. He decided to drive for Uber at night, knowing he would make cash that would add to his other savings and make it possible for him to pay her tuition with cash. While driving, he had fun, talked to his rides, and made the most of what could potentially be a menial job.

He had the mindset of a person who's built a multimillion-dollar business, but he took an Uber job so his daughter could attend an Ivy League school. He was willing to do whatever it took to get her there and he wasn't complaining that Harvard charges a high tuition, or that he had to work nights after a long day at his business to make the money he needed.

His mindset was nothing short of amazing. These two Uber drivers are examples of the voices in your head. These two people tell totally different stories about their experience, totally different stories about what they're doing.

How we talk to ourselves can be trained through tactical and tangible things you can do. Start writing positive thoughts down today and retrain your brain.

## Tactical and Tangible Things You Can Do

I personally don't like journaling, but I have found that the fastest way to learn how to turn the stories in my brain that tell me I'm not good enough or that no one is ever going to pay me much, or who the hell am I to think that I could possibly do this, is to write down better thoughts.

Your brain has said all those things to you so many times that you don't even catch it. I know that the best way to catch the voices in your head is to write them down. I know it feels weird to remove yourself from your own brain, but it works. Simply take a piece of paper and write whatever your goal is; for example: sign ten clients this month OR sign a new client by the end of the week. Just write down everything that comes up.

Take your time. Maybe you're thinking, *That's impossible. Nobody's ever going to pay me. I don't know how I'm going to make success happen.* That's going to come up first. I know this to be true because there's not a person out there who has not thought about those things. The difference between them and you is that you can choose which one of the stories to continue to tell yourself. I know. I've done it. I don't continue to tell myself, *there's no way in hell I can be a success*. I now tell myself, *well, yeah, there's not a lot of people running really successful businesses. I better be willing to do more or do something different than those people.*

It's the most tangible, tactical thing I can tell you to do when it comes to catching those voices in your head: write all of it down.

I'm a student at Brooke Castillo's Life Coach School and a student of her Self-Coaching Scholars. Brooke calls this practice of writing it all down a thought download. You "download" all those awful thoughts that are spinning around in your head.

It really helped me catch those sneaky stories that I tell myself. Try it and then you get to decide (once you're aware of the thoughts) how you can catch them. Caution: your brain can think all kinds of thoughts when you let it happen on autopilot, which is what your brain loves to do. The thoughts just kind of cruise right on by. *Yep, I'm not worthy. Not good enough. Success is never going to happen for me. I can't make the level of sales I want. I don't have the secret code for success.*

Once you write this nonsense down, the next time your brain wants to serve that up, you're going to notice it. You're gonna respond with *No, No, No*. That's not the story you're telling yourself anymore. The story you're telling yourself is this: *I'm good enough. Of course people would pay me because I'm really good at what I do.* Those conversations are literally the only difference between successful people and people who never become successful.

10

# FOCUS ON WHAT YOU CAN CONTROL

Sometimes when you're selling, you may start thinking that you are working with zero control over your desired outcomes. Sales may or may not happen, but you have little actual control over that. When you come to this realization, something else can happen.

You start giving away the actual power you DO have. Reminder: Your power comes from knowing you are an important businessperson who does not give all your power to someone else.

## You Can Control Your Actions, Reactions, and How You Show Up

You're still thinking, *But I can't make people buy from me. I can't make people say yes. I can't make them give me their credit card. I can't make them sign the contract. I can't make them take action.*

You are one hundred percent correct. You cannot make

anyone do anything they don't want to do. Because we have talked so much in this book about power and taking your power back, the best way to do that is to focus on what you can control.

While you cannot control what other people do, you can control what you do. You can control the actions you take every day. You can ask yourself the question: if I want to sign ten clients this month, what actions can I control?

You can control the content you post on social media, how much, and how you show up. You can control the number of new people you connect with. You can control how many people you invite to coffee chats. You can control how many people you invite to sales conversations. What else? How many networking events you attend, how many friends and family you ask for help, how many emails you plan to send. You can control how many phone calls to make, what social media platform to show up on. If you go live on Facebook, you can control how you show up. You can control a whole host of things.

What you like to do instead is say, *well, I can't control that person over there, so I'm just not going to do anything.* Turn that around to the only way that you're successful in business is to focus on what you can control, which are your own actions.

We also talked previously about sales being a numbers game, not in a negative way, not in a throw-spaghetti-at-a-wall-and-see-what-sticks kind of way, but in the law of averages kind of way. If you talk to enough people, the more people who know what you do, the more money you make.

If you are overwhelmed, consider this: make a plan, specifically a sales plan.

In Social Sellers Academy, which is where we train sales reps for seven and eight figure CEOs, we talk about time management, metrics and numbers, and metrics tracker. What I highly recommend is having a plan for your activity, having your networking power hour on your calendar.

You can control putting that on your calendar. You can control how you show up to network, too. You get to decide if you're going to reach out to 25 people in a Facebook group today and invite them to your upcoming webinar.

This is what that would look like: first, decide how many clients you want per month. Let's say the number is ten clients. So, if you close 30% of the people you book calls with, you will need to book thirty-five people on sales calls per month to get ten clients.

This is called sales math. It's what you do to hit your numbers, which is important if you want consistent cash flow in your business. It's not hard to do, but it is super important.

Back to the example: you decide you want ten clients and know that you need to schedule thirty-five sales calls. How many invitations to sales calls do you need to get thirty-five calls booked? You need to reach out to at least seventy people because you know that 50% of the people you ask will say no.

Great. Do you see how we're working backwards to your goal? How many new conversations do you make to get seventy people to say yes to a sales conversation? That number might be close to 300. You can control getting into 300 conversations that lead to seventy sales call invitations. You can control your conversion rate on sales calls because you set yourself up for success.

You just used sales math to figure out what it will take for your business to succeed. Now you know your numbers.

Before you did the sales math, you thought that sales happened by accident. And now you know that it takes effort, but you can control that effort.

Always concentrate on the actions that you can take and the things that you can control. When you do, all sorts of opportunities pop up. What's fun is that the result doesn't always correlate to the action.

This is a little mind-bending, but when you start taking action, opportunities present themselves. They don't always come directly from the action. They come from making the decision to take the action. So do ones that you generated yourself, but know that you will see possibilities showing up that were not part of your plan.

Let's go back to the math. You plan to make seventy invitations to sales calls over the course of a month. If you work twenty days a month, you need to make four invitations to sales calls every day. You can control that. You are in total and complete control of that. That is a specific activity that you can focus on.

A lot of you spend your time asking, *where am I going to find these people? What if they're not qualified? What if they don't have any money?*

It doesn't matter. You can't control those things.

You can get better at learning that you have no control over their finances. The more that you deal with this, the better the thinking that you use, the better you will get at handling the ones who are not going to buy from you.

This is helpful thinking: *I'm gonna go out and start conversations with fifty new people, and I'm going to invite four of them to a sales conversation. I can control that. I am in total and complete control of it. Social media gives us an open door to billions of people. You can't tell me that I can't find fifty people to start conversations with on social media today. I am in control of my actions.*

When you think of success in the sales world, or in the business world, what are you in control of that builds that success? You are in control of the actions that you take. There are a lot of people out there that teach you to sit and wait: sit and wait for people to reach out to you, sit and wait for somebody to raise their hand, sit and wait for somebody to drop into your sales funnel. Sure, it works for some people. I know that there are people that have very successful businesses that are making a lot of money doing that. Good for them. Ask them how much money they're spending for that to work.

I can tell you that they're spending a ton of money to make sure enough people jump into their funnel. You, as the sales rep or the new entrepreneur, don't want to sit and wait.

You want to go out and take action, maybe through networking events, maybe through networking in Facebook groups, maybe through joining coaching programs. Use whatever works best, but know that you are in control of the action that you take every single day. You are in control of the number of new people you meet and talk to.

You are in control of the number of sales conversations that you make. You are in complete and total control of those things as long as you realize that you must take control of those things and take action every day. When you do, your success is inevitable.

## Your Reactions – You're in Control of Them, Too

Using my example from before, if you need to make seventy invitations to sales calls, knowing that half of them will be a no, that doesn't sound like a lot of fun, right? It sounds like work with not a great ROI, for one thing.

But what if you were to decide that you're not going to let

this derail your whole day? You can decide to make yet another invitation to a sales call to finish your daily sales activity.

You can be mad that somebody says no, and more than a little frustrated. Your feelings can be hurt. You can be embarrassed. But what if, at the same time, you get to say, *I'm working my system. I'm taking action. I need and want to make four invites to sales calls.* You can do all of that.

You can control how you react to the situation. The best way I know to control your reactions is to anticipate the noes you're going to get and be okay with that. Because if you need to make five invitations to sales calls every single day, you know that at least two of them are going to be a no. Be prepared for that.

A shift happens. When you get a no, it's not the end of the world. You're not devastated. You're not miserable. You're thinking that it sucks, but you're not getting emotionally tied to that thought. You also know that you have three more chances today, so you keep on going.

This happened to one of my sales reps who sent a direct message. She wrote, *Hi! I just wanted to get to know you and invite you to this upcoming workshop. We're loving the business that you've built so far. I think you would see a lot of value in this workshop.*

The woman came back with, *No thanks. I'm not interested.* My rep then asked her, *are you interested in having a successful sales team?*

She came back, *Well, not one that is fishing for leads in the direct messages.* That was her response. *Not one that's fishing for leads in the direct messages.*

My sales rep sent her reply to me, and I asked my rep, "How do you feel about her response?" She thought about it for a second and said, "She's not our people."

If this were your story, your reaction could be, *Yeah, well, phishing and sending DMs to people to build relationships is bad on social media.* No, you tell yourself, *They're just not my people.*

My rep was not mad or offended. She did not let feel dejected or let that derail her entire day. Instead, she chose to say, *No, she's just not my people.*

My people, my people, our people – you are building relationships because that's what you do. That's what social media is meant for. That's what your people believe. You're not going to get your panties in a wad over someone who doesn't believe what you believe. Because my rep was able to control her reaction to a somewhat negative response, she did not derail her entire day. She just reminded herself that the prospect was not her person and moved on to other women to message.

So many people would have let that response stop them in their tracks and not allow themselves to move forward. There's something wrong with you because one random person on the internet doesn't like the DMs.

I'm not saying that you won't have bad days. It does not mean that you never get frustrated or angry, or your feelings get hurt. You're human and that happens. How long you choose to sit in that negative emotion is up to you.

The only two things you can control are your actions and reactions. When you get a response that you don't like, don't become a robot. Decide how long you are going to let the response derail you. And then, how long are you going to wait before you start taking action again?

It's small stuff, but these are the things you control. You can control the action that you're willing to take and you can control how you're going to react. Again, some days are going to be better than others, but realize that you don't have to be angry. You don't have to be upset. You don't have to feel rejected. You don't have to feel disappointed. You're going to give yourself five minutes to feel disappointed. You're going to get a cup of coffee. Then you're going to keep taking action. That is all that you can do.

## How You Show Up in the World

How you show up in the world is one of my favorite things to talk about. Social media is one way you can decide how to show up. I talk fast and I talk with my hands and I'm very expressive in a lot of ways. I get to choose that. That's how I show up in the world. I show up as myself.

The number one comment on my YouTube videos is people wishing that I would slow down. I know those commenters are not my people.

Would it be better if I spoke a little slower? Probably. Am I going to slow down because one or two strangers on the internet think I talk too fast? No, I am not.

I get to control how I show up on the internet, how much of my story I'm willing to share, and the person that I want to be perceived as. I'm in control of the type of content that I post, how I show up in coffee chats, how I show up on Facebook Lives, and how I show up in this book. I don't get to control people's opinions of it. I only control how I show up.

I am often told that I'm the person who talks too fast. The person who talks with her hands. The person who is direct and has strong opinions and has no problem telling people when I disagree with them. That's just who I am. I don't have to be anybody that I am not, but I get to control how I show up. I get to control the image of myself that I want to portray. Some people think that it's a bad thing. I think it's amazing.

You can't control other people. You can't control their minds. You can't control their budgets. You can't control their wallets. You can't force them to give you money. You can't force them to get in a sales conversation with you.

You can control your actions, and you can control how you show up. Show up as the best version of yourself every day.

# 11

## PEOPLE + NUMBERS

### Why Are the Numbers Important?

New businesspeople tend to have a love-hate relationship with sales numbers. When you talk about people in terms of numbers, it feels uncomfortably impersonal. Remember that businesses are all about people and the numbers. While I understand that it feels impersonal, numbers are absolutely necessary to talk about and to pay attention to.

People resist managing their numbers because it's not their favorite part of running their business. It's the least sexy part of running a business, but numbers are the roadmap for signing clients. If you don't pay attention to the numbers, it will always be a guessing game as to where your next client is coming from.

As Kelly Roach says, "What gets measured gets managed."

The numbers become important because they give you a roadmap. That's when revenue becomes predictable, and profit becomes predictable, because you know what the formula is. If you never take the time to learn the numbers and track the numbers, you don't know what the formula is.

That becomes a constant struggle to troubleshoot. Sales is a combination of fixed numbers and some variables. The fixed numbers you derive using sales math, which we talked about in Chapter 10. While sales is a giant experiment, the problem is that so many of you are playing with the variables only and there's never anything fixed to compare to your variable. You have not tracked your numbers to know that, for example, it takes thirty-five sales calls to get ten terrific clients. Those are fixed numbers.

All these variables start to create frustration, overwhelm, and unpredictability. The numbers are not sexy and they're not fun, but they are mission critical to business success. And this is true across the board, no matter what type of business you own.

You might think, *oh, well I'm brand new.* Or, *oh, you know, my goal isn't that big* or, *oh, I don't really need to track this.*

But I promise you, if you figure out how to track your sales numbers in the beginning, it will be easier as the numbers get bigger. The reason why I can confidently say that is because in the beginning, my numbers were low. I didn't feel the need to track them. I didn't think it was any big deal to track them.

I was wrong.

At some point in time, you're going to want to grow and scale like I did. You're going to want to go from a couple thousand dollars to tens of thousands of dollars to hopefully millions of dollars in your business. I could only achieve my own success by starting to track my sales numbers.

If you can learn the discipline of tracking your numbers

when you're small, it will be easier to scale and grow. You want to do things like hire a team and make an impact, make donations, and do all the things that are important to you.

When there's a predictable revenue in your business, that's when you can live a bigger life that pays for all the things you want and need. Paying for all your projects happens because you can now rely on the money coming in to pay for it.

I get it. Doing the sales math and tracking all the numbers is nobody's favorite thing. It's not my favorite thing. I literally lead a sales training organization and it is not my favorite thing, but it is one hundred percent necessary.

How do you make it your favorite thing? You link it to something you love.

Here's an example: let's say you were trying to train for a marathon. The marathon, which is 26.2 miles long, is in sixteen weeks. This simple math allows you to know the exact number of miles you need to run every single week to prepare for that race.

Training may not be something you enjoy. There will be days when you wake up and don't want to run. There will be days where you are sore. There will be days when you are tired. There will be days where you have blisters on your feet. There are days when it is cold and rainy. The last thing you want to do is run those five miles... or those fifteen miles.

It is the exact same in business. You would never set out to run those 26.2 miles without a plan unless you're a super athlete already, and then, game on. Generally speaking, the average human who runs marathons does not do it without a plan. They know how many miles they have to run each day and every week to be able to wake up on race day and run 26.2 miles.

How does that not favorite thing become your favorite thing? You need to know that the work that you're doing every single day, whether you like it or not, is getting you closer to your goal. Sometimes there are activities that you must do that you don't enjoy. How do you talk yourself into it? You focus on where you're going.

You tell yourself that if you track your numbers, it's going to get you to your six-figure business, to your $10,000 commission check, or to reach success as a seven-figure business, whatever you're hoping to achieve. Make it your favorite thing by tying it to success.

It also takes the guesswork out of it on the days when you just don't feel like you can do and be your business. If you don't know your numbers regularly, the number of days you don't feel like doing your numbers can be huge. Figure out what you're going to do today. If you're not into figuring out your numbers, but know exactly what you need to do, you can muscle through it, get it done, and move on.

I also want to clarify to you that numbers are important. The numbers don't have to be fancy either. An Excel spreadsheet is fine. Please don't overcomplicate this. Do not use the excuse of having to find a new CRM and build all these tracking systems and spreadsheets because that's not progress, that's procras-tination.

I've told this story a million times. In 2018, I spent the entire year getting ready to get ready. I did all the things. I remember telling myself, *I'm going to do this and I'm going to learn that.* That's what we tend to do when it comes to tracking our numbers. For my leads, I found an app that worked for me. Don't do what I did. Just open an Excel spreadsheet. Put the days of the week down the side or across the top and start tracking.

## What Numbers Should You Be Tracking?

This is going to be a little bit different depending on where you are in your business. I teach the Power Hour Strategy to my clients. This process was born out of necessity because I was growing my first business alongside a full-time job. I didn't have a lot of time. I had to be very specific about how I spent it, so I developed this straightforward strategy that is essentially just like networking. It's a very specific hour in your day that is dedicated to networking online. For many of you, tracking your Power Hour activity is important. What you track are how many comments, likes, and how much engagement you are giving and getting on posts.

For some of you who are doing more, if you're a salesperson or you just are doing more lead generation type activity and messaging campaigns or cold outreach, you might not need to track your power hour. For me, what I'm ultimately trying to do is develop a formula, which is called sales math, that helps you get to signed clients. What I like to track is how many new people you are talking to every single day. You also track how many conversations you have moving forward.

Doing this helps you see two things: 1) Are you talking to the same twenty people over and over again? Or 2) Are you adding new people and not pushing them through the sales funnel and converting them as clients? Basically, you need to track how many new people you're talking to every day, but you also want to track the quality of the people you're tracking so you can move conversations along, however that makes sense for you and your business.

As I said, if you are working on your Power Hour and focusing on outreach like email or phone calls, you need to track how many new people you are reaching out to every single day, how many you are connecting with, and how many existing conversations you move forward. These are all important metrics.

Managing the metrics can feel like walking a tightrope, though. First, numbers are dry. Second, I recommend that you track the numbers of qualified people. You may go out and talk to fifty new people every single day, but not all those people are actually going to be your people.

You know that of those fifty people, only twenty of them are qualified in some capacity. There are a lot of ways to define qualified. It might be qualified from what you can learn about them online. You can go look at somebody's profile and think, *hey, this person is qualified.* As in, once you learn a little bit more about this person, they fit the criteria of somebody who would buy your products or services.

You also need to make sure that you're building a database of qualified people. You're tracking new people and you're moving conversations forward. Ultimately, then, you're tracking a qualified database.

You want to be adding people to your qualified database every single day, but it starts with strangers. Talk to new people, get into conversations, and learn what makes them qualified to you. Ask yourself if they are great additions to your database. Your qualified database is arguably the most valuable asset that you have as a business owner and as a salesperson, because your qualified database contains the people that you are going to build relationships with and persist with until they become clients, or they tell you no.

So, you're tracking qualified people and moving them through the funnel. These people are qualified based on what you learn about them, either online or in conversation. Then you want to track your invitations to conversations. Some of you might track your networking calls or your connect calls on the front end. Some of you might make an invitation directly to a sales conversation. Whatever process works best for you is perfectly fine.

I personally like the connect call, or the coffee chat, or the networking call. It's a softer ask. It's an easier task. Depending on who your ideal client is, they may not want to hop on a connect call. As an example, if you are calling on high level CEOs, they are just not going to get on the phone and BS with you. If you need to, you're going to have to ask to hop on a sales call. If you're inviting both types of calls, track the invitations to both types of calls because you want to know how many invitations it takes to get a call booked.

You're starting new conversations and now you need to track the movement of qualified leads through the sales funnel and into your database. How many people are getting into your qualified database? You always want to know your sales math. You want to know how many invitations it takes to book a call. Then you need to know how many calls it takes for you to get a client. So, not a lot of numbers that you need to track, but you need to know them consistently day in and day out.

## Understanding Sales Math

Sales math can show you something like this: it takes you talking to a hundred new people to wind up with thirty qualified people in your database to wind up with ten connect calls, two sales calls, and one client. Bringing all these numbers together is very important in the beginning. If you're new to tracking, new to sales, or you are in a new sales role, your numbers may not be the best.

But you're tracking the numbers to create predictability, and you're tracking them to see and encourage improvement. In the beginning, it might take a hundred leads. Eventually it'll get to eighty and the hope is that it gets to sixty, and for every sixty leads you bring into your ecosystem, you sign one client. Whether it's you, whether it's your sales team, whether you're hiring someone, or whether you're bringing on a virtual assistant to do the networking for you, you will know the formula that is needed to get clients into your business.

If you show up and work with this formula every single day, you will make money. It takes away all the guesswork, all the frustration, all the headaches. Sales math also helps you understand and make projections in your business. Examples include how many days it takes to sell this many clients, and how much money you make in the process. Those are fun things that happen as a result of sales math. You can then raise your thinking, pick bigger goals to reach. Ask yourself, how can you grow? How do you scale? Can you raise your rates? How many more people should you hire? Can you invest more in ads?

The magic really happens once you really understand your sales math. Like I said earlier, there are so many people who struggle with this because they don't want to identify people as numbers. I am never proposing that people are only numbers, but at the end of the day, you have to know how many people you need in your world to build and grow your business. This is data collection, analysis about how well you are getting in front of potential clients, and how you serve the number of people you ultimately need for your business to be a success.

Entrepreneurship is the best personal development tool you'll ever have. Yes, I'm saying that again. This extra layer of numbers bolsters you. There is not a successful businessperson out there that doesn't understand their numbers to some capacity. Not as many people talk about sales numbers as talk about marketing numbers. But here, we're talking sales numbers.

For instance, you might have heard that you can expect 46% of the people who registered for your webinar to show up. Out of the 46%, you can expect between two and 5% of registrants to actually enroll, if they're the right people. We hear numbers like these all the time and people have no problem tracking them. When it comes to actual sales numbers, though, we get a little overwhelmed.

To me, this is just the next step. It also makes it so you're not in a place where you're ever dependent upon a webinar or a launch because you have a true sales funnel. That's the difference between a sales funnel and a marketing funnel. You know your numbers and you understand what they look like. This creates predictability that prevents you from being dependent on outside sources like webinars.

Now, this doesn't mean that you're not running ads to bring people into your ecosystem. There are a million ways to do that. It doesn't have to just be cold outreach. It could be podcast interviews. It could be guest expert training in people's Facebook groups. It can be Facebook ads or live on Facebook and inviting people to book a call. It can be live speaking. Some of my first clients came to me from speaking live. Whatever platform you're using to bring people into your ecosystem is totally fine. It's just understanding what happens once they get into the ecosystem.

## An Example Showing Why Sales Math Is SO Important

I will be honest: at the beginning of my sales career, I hated the numbers' part. I remember telling myself, *I don't want to do this*. My whole career was all about not wanting to do this. Then I realized I wasn't getting the results I wanted through the activity that I was taking. I had no way of troubleshooting. I knew that was because I had no data to tell me what was and wasn't working.

When I became an entrepreneur, I went back to the drawing board, back to what I knew worked. I came up with the Power Hour and literally chose to talk to twenty-five people every day. From there, I was able to go into a Facebook group and get involved in twenty-five conversations, and I could pull at least ten of those people into the DMS. I could pull at least five of those people into my Facebook group. I realized, Eureka! This is just a different version of knowing your numbers.

My client, Melissa McClung, has embraced sales math in a way that has been life-changing for her family. Melissa stays home with her two kids and at the writing of this book, she and her husband are in the process of adopting baby number three.

One of the things that Melissa has done incredibly well since she came into my world was recognizing that she was okay with numbers, and actually good with them. She also understood what they told her about her business. She has not reached millions and millions of dollars in revenue because that's not Melissa's goal.

But what it has created for her is predictability. Melissa knows if she gets on LinkedIn and connects with fifty new people every day, a predictable percentage of people would accept her connection request. She would start conversations with them and get them specifically into sales conversations. She got to the point where she knew exactly how many people she needed to initiate a conversation with to book a sales call and convert them to clients.

Melissa sells a high-ticket, one-to-one offer. She likes to sign six clients a month and she knows exactly how to do that. She has done it so well that she was able to hire a VA to do the connection requests for her. She fine-tuned her business to the point where it is now predictable.

Those hours for Melissa were not her worrying about getting more money and more clients, they were about more time with her kids. They were about time spent with her spouse. Really understanding those numbers and creating that predictability has created this fantastic funnel and Melissa knows what levers to pull.

It comes back to the idea of how many connection requests are sent, how many will be accepted, how many conversations get turned into voice-to-voice communications? How many of those voice messages will then turn into clients?

Through all that increase in confidence, Melissa has also raised the price of her program about five-fold. She has the same number of clients, but significantly more cash because she's got more confidence. She's signed more clients and she gets results. Don't forget that the better you get at what you do, the more you can charge for it.

Melissa has a hundred percent success rate as a career coach and she's incredible at what she does. She offers a money-back guarantee in which she will work with you until she can place you in a job.

What's also cool is she knows when to push pause as she prepares to bring a new baby into their family. She will be able to put a pin in the business while the family and baby are first together, and then pull the pin out when she is ready to restart her business.

# 12

## REAP WHAT YOU SOW

Reap what you sow is based on the thirty-day rule, a technique that I learned from a gentleman named Jeb Blount, the author of *Fanatical Prospecting*.

What I learned by reading Jeff's book is that the work you do in the next thirty days is what feeds you in ninety days.

### Let's Start with Persistence

This is why persistence is so important. The reason that sales teams and business owners in general struggle is because you can't keep a full pipeline of leads, which is due to a lack of persistence. When you are willing to chase a lead for a week, two weeks, three weeks, four weeks and beyond, you get clients, but in the process, you may also get bored.

What you need to know are two important facts. First and foremost, the data online is telling us that it can take between thirty and fifty touch points before somebody pays attention to your marketing messages. It takes this much effort, especially if they do not know you, a complete stranger coming at them cold, and they don't know your brand or business.

That's number one. Number two: let's use Chet Holmes' statistic once more that at any given time only 3% of our ecosystem is in the market to buy. Those two pieces of information tell us that persistence is arguably the most important thing in sales. Because most people aren't willing to do the thirty to fifty touches, and most people are frustrated by a 3% success rate, what happens over the course of those ninety days? People will continue to change course. They will do something for two or three weeks, not see tremendous results, and quit.

Two or three weeks won't get them the results they want. They will then move on and try something else for two or three weeks. It may look like, *Oh, I'm networking on Facebook. Oh, now I'm on Instagram, too. Oh, now I'm over on LinkedIn and now I'm over here, and now I'm over there. I changed my business name and my Facebook Group name and I'm gonna change my offer and I'm gonna change my pricing.*

You can take on forty-seven different iterations of your business and still have zero to few clients to show for it. Be honest with yourself – you just never worked the full funnel. That is the 90-day rule of business.

When my clients come to me and they want to make a change in what they're doing, I'll ask them, "Have you done it for ninety days? Because the work that you were doing today is going to feed you in ninety days. If you keep changing the work and strategy and you keep changing the approach and you keep changing what you're doing, you're dead in the water."

That looks like you never giving one project, one process, or one strategy an opportunity to work. I would say all the strategies work. Just like there are a million books on sales and a million books on marketing, there are a million ways to sign clients.

We are lucky to live in a world where there are so many options to connect with new people and solve problems for them. The problem is that most of you have a giant persistence problem, and you wind up getting bored.

Persistence is really being able to take that one lead, that one person who you would love to get in front of, and reach out through a variety of touchpoints, including engaging them on social media, commenting on their Instagram stories, sending them an email or a handwritten note, and be willing to get their attention for ninety days or longer.

Remember, only 3% of our people are ready to buy right now, which means 97% are not. Out of every 100 people in your ecosystem, 97 of them are not ready to buy. Or they plan to hire someone with your services in the next quarter, so knowing you now increases your chances of getting them as a client. The problem is that you're not persistent enough in pursuing that relationship. Even though they're not ready to buy that, they may be once they learn about you.

Much of your lack of persistence is because you're worried what other people will think of you. Stop thinking that you are stalking them or annoying them or being pushy. You need to hold to that script, the one that says people are going to live with the problem that you can solve for them if you refuse to be persistent with your help and follow through by following up.

This is not about reaching out to somebody every single day. This isn't about being annoying, but being prepared for, once or twice a week, showing up in this person's social media feed with a comment. You need to create an air of familiarity around them in order to get them as a client.

Most of us don't have the discipline and persistence because the blessing that is the internet gives us an endless supply of leads. Why would you persist with a single person? Especially if your four outreaches do not turn the person into a client?

How do you stay in the mindset of persistence? You must come at it understanding a few things. First and foremost, I like to believe that every single person on the internet is a willing and capable adult who can handle the no-thank-you-I'm-not-interested replies that come to them.

If the person you reached out to did not want what you had to offer, they can tell you and that's okay. Really, it's okay. I also let people who reach out to me know that I'm not interested in what they have to offer so they can move along and talk to other people. That way, they can discontinue direct messaging me over and over again when I have no intentions of talking to them, much less hiring them.

The second mindset issue I want you to understand is how we all consume information and media today. There is a ton of it. Think about what your inbox looks like and how loud and crazy social media can be and then think about your busy day at any given time. It's busy, busy, busy all around you.

So many messages are coming at you, so consider people you are reaching out to. The number of messages that are coming at people at any given time makes it hard for them to balance their work life and respond to you immediately. When someone doesn't message you back, it probably means they're busy. It's not because of a lack of interest, but at some point in time it becomes too overwhelming for them to go through their messages right away.

I know I said two mindset thoughts, but here's a third, and it may be the idea you want to read the least, but it's true: Most people aren't willing to be persistent. I will tell you as somebody who had both CEO and Former Director as my LinkedIn title, I receive a lot of direct messages. The number of people who reach out once or twice and then go away is alarming. They'll call once or twice, and they'll go away because lazy salespeople everywhere have trained them that way.

When I'm selling, I am willing to be persistent. Having a conversation with you is important to me. The people I'm reaching out to are going to be way more likely to give me their time because of my persistence. When people are reaching out to me, I am much more willing to give my time to somebody who follows up. When they don't, my thought is, *you must not believe in what you do. You must not be that passionate about helping me. You must not see that much value in solving my problem if all you're willing to do is reach out to me once or twice.*

Here is the thinking of people you reach out to again and again over the course of several weeks: they need to know what you have to offer.

My mindset of persistence is based on my passion and belief in the work I do and my clients' results. It is my duty to get your attention even if you say no thank you, I'm not interested, or I'm not your person.

I know that if you can be persistent, then you can be interesting and interested in them while providing value that eventually gets you on their calendar for a real conversation.

But most of you never get to that point. You have not developed the mindset that keeps your passion top of mind. Your mindset needs to remind you that it's your job and your team's follow up. That's vital to getting your prospects' attention and start forming relationships with them.

Persistence does not sound like this: *Are you ready yet? Are you ready yet? Are you ready yet? You want to buy something?*

Instead, say something simple like, "Hey Mary, it looks like you and your family took a great vacation. I hope it was fun. You know, I was thinking about you the other day. I see that you're launching your program in a few weeks. We just put out this amazing podcast I think you're going to find super valuable. Here's the link. Good luck. Hope it goes great."

It's reading somebody's Instagram caption and leaving a thoughtful comment, not just a comment like *love this* and a heart emoji. Instead, it's, *hey, this is super insightful. Thank you for sharing this.* It looks like sending a handwritten note or a lovely birthday card. The attention is coming from all different angles. It's being creative and it's being human.

I have a sales rep on my team who was in the process of booking a sales call with someone to whom she sent eight direct messages over the course of several weeks. Eight messages. All ignored. Then she sent a message about the woman's nephew who graduated from college: *Congratulations! That's so exciting. Were you able to attend in person?*

Suddenly, the woman had so much to say. Finally, it became a two-way conversation. It was after this that my sales rep pulled it back around to inviting her to a sales conversation. You never know what the thing is that you're going to say or what question you're going to ask that's going to be a person's gateway.

That is the power of persistence. The reason that people don't like salespeople is because salespeople try to force their agendas and their timelines onto the buyer because they need to make a sale. They don't consider that they're talking to a human who would respond favorably to a thoughtful comment on their social media post, or a lovely birthday card they receive in the mail.

## And Now Let's Talk About Patience

If you have your sales math figured out, you'll be fine taking the prospecting slow and steady. Help yourself get clients by not focusing entirely on the math but focusing on relationships and solving problems. Yes, of course you would love for that deal to close today. Does it matter if it closes today or next month or the month after that? Not when you have your sales math figured out.

You have to practice patience because you will, as soon as you get somebody engaged in a conversation, go directly into booking a sales call. You forget that people buy on their own timelines, for their own reasons, not your reasons.

It's my job as a business owner or a salesperson to walk this person through the process and then have the patience to allow them to arrive in the place where they're ready to buy.

I should add a giant asterisk to this because I know you tend to use your lack of patience as an excuse to not ask, "Hey, are you ready to buy yet? Hey, is it time? Hey, let's go ahead and get on a call."

Let me give you a perfect example. One of my team members was in a conversation with someone who was interested in what we do but put the brakes on things. We suspected it was a cash flow issue. She told us they might have to wait a couple of months and offered a few more things that prevented her commitment right away.

I don't believe in convincing, and I don't believe in arm twist-ing. It's not my jam. What I recommend you do in this situation is to read between the lines, and be able to say, "This is just an objection. This is just a stall. I need to patiently walk this person through why waiting several months to fix a sales problem in their business could potentially cost them tens of thousands, if not hundreds of thousands of dollars."

I'm not saying you don't overcome objections. What I'm saying is that sometimes when your prospect says, "I'm looking at buying in Q4," don't be a pain in the ass and arm twist them into buying in Q2 or Q3. Persistence is important, but you also have to practice patience.

The idea that only 3% of people are needing what you sell means those other 97% aren't ready right now, or maybe ever. You must be patient with them and build a relationship. You cannot rush relationships either.

I know that can be hard to understand because you've met lots of people who you became besties with almost immediately after meeting them. Then there are those you've met five or six times and decided you really didn't like them that much, but once you get to know them, you think they're amazing.

Sales is a lot like this – not everyone is your ideal client. People who reach out to you may not love you right away because they don't know how amazing you are yet. Over time, with a patient attitude, they learn that you are. We've all met that person who has been way too pushy and impatient, or the sales rep who tried to push their agenda onto you, which instantly turns you off. Don't be that person.

Know that there is a balance between persistence and patience. What I want to teach you is this idea of considering whose agenda you are selling to. And you are probably think-

THE 100K SALES METHOD

ing, *Ryan, it's always my agenda. I'm the one that's trying to sell them something.*

You're only trying to sell them something if they have the problem that you solve. Yes, it is your ultimate agenda to sell something. But it is also your job and duty to solve a problem for them, too. You must always put the client first and be sensitive about timing. Is this the timeframe they told you to follow up in? Did they say they're going on vacation for two weeks? How long after they came back from vacation, took a breath, and dug through their inbox were you in touch, asking for a sale?

When somebody tells you to follow up with them on Monday, don't follow up with them on Monday at 8:00 AM. Let them have a cup of coffee. Think about selling as a way to draw them to you rather than trying to force the sale. Going back to the concept of the 90-day rule, you have to understand that you can't speed the ninety days up by being a pest. You must follow the process.

You have to follow a process, be persistent, interesting, and engaging, but then you have to give people solutions to their problems. Please, marry patience and persistence. How do you get to the point where you can marry persistence and patience? When you know the sales process.

I know my numbers and I know what activity is going to bring clients into Social Sellers Academy. We teach a system we call Daily Sales on Demand. It is meant to create daily sales in your business. What I've talked about in the last two chapters is what creates those daily sales on demand. If you know your numbers, are persistent and patient with your numbers, you will have a business that generates as many sales as you want it to.

The biggest mistake new entrepreneurs make is impatience,

which leads to frustration and boredom. It shows up when you change course after four or six weeks or reach out to somebody three or four times and move on. You look for the low-hanging fruit instead of working the system. The sales get wider and further apart and before you know it, you're back to where you were, which was not a consistent sales situation. What you create is a cycle of frustration and this cycle never closes anything.

I want to be clear with you that I'm not proposing you bang your head against the wall. I'm not proposing that you do a bunch of outreach to strangers on the internet. Everything that we have talked about in these past two chapters has to be done strategically and intentionally. Remember, we talked about finding qualified people in your sales navigation. Those are the people you're persistent with. Those are the people who you're being patient with while at the same time continuing to add more and more people to your ecosystem. The number of clients you need is dependent on how the system works for you.

I know that you may be a little overwhelmed right now. You're like, "Wow. I have to talk to how many people?" If you are a sales rep for an organization, the expectation is you close ten to 100 deals every month. Your activity level is way higher than a done-for-you agency that only has room for ten clients a quarter, so you have to take these numbers and the system and adjust it to your output.

Yes, it's a numbers game and yes, you have to be persistent and yes, you have to be patient. We work with a client inside of Social Sellers Academy who offers contracts that are $150,000 each. She needs ten clients per year. For her, she must find a very small and niched pool of people and build rock solid relationships with them. We also have people in the Academy who sell things that are $3,000 and they need way more leads. They're not going quite as deep with relationship building for a $3,000 sale. One of my favorite things about sales and about business is that you can turn the dial based on your personal needs.

You must practice patience both with yourself and your buyer. Think through this 90-day rule and let it show you how well it works.

# 13

## TALENT VERSUS HARD WORK

There is a giant misconception that you've all heard about sales-people. It's the myth that they are "born" salespeople. When you say the word sales, you have a very specific person in mind and that person is an extrovert. They're a person who likes people and they like to be around people. They like to talk a lot and they like to be the center of attention. So many people think about salespeople they've met before and think, *Oh, no, I'm not a salesperson. I'm not good at sales.*

Let's examine this and start with this thought: there is not a toddler in the world that's not good at sales. Go find me a three- or four-year-old who is not the best negotiator you have ever met in your life. They will not take no for an answer. Toddlers use survival skills to get what they need at the moment. Their behavior is innate because it's necessary.

That leads me to this: we are all born salespeople. At some point in your life, you became conditioned to think that sales are bad and you're not capable. Not true. Sales is a skill you can learn. It's not a personality trait. It's not specific to extroverts. It's not specific to people who like to be around people. It's not specific to people who like to be the center of attention. Selling is actually about helping someone get a specific result.

## Sales Is a Skill You Can Learn

Sales is easy to learn and there is a specific process that you follow. You may think that good salespeople are about their personality traits. I would argue that good salespeople are actually the opposite of what you think. Good salespeople are great connectors and great listeners. Good salespeople tend to be empathetic. Good salespeople tend to be service driven. Good salespeople tend to be passionate about what they sell and what they do. All of that is the exact opposite of what you think makes a good salesperson.

Even if you are an introvert, you can still be an excellent salesperson. In fact, I think introverts make excellent salespeople because they are great listeners and are very good at one-on-one relationships.

As far as I'm concerned, learning how to sell is just learning a process: questions we should ask, and how to run excellent consultation calls or discovery calls. It's about learning how to ask good questions to overcome objections.

Sales is not about a personality trait. It's not something you're born with. If you really want to take the time to learn it, it's very easy to do. People who are attracted to sales are people who like to be around other people. They don't want a job where they sit at their desk all day long. They want to be out and about meeting people and have an experience of talking to a lot of different people all day, every day. Sales jobs and sales job descriptions wind up attracting a specific type of person, but that person isn't necessarily the best at sales.

We have covered throughout this book that sales is about relationships, bottom line. Are you genuinely interested in getting to know people and helping them get a specific result? Then you will be excellent at sales because you can learn the sales process, the anatomy of a sales call. You can learn what questions to ask to overcome objections. You can learn how to generate leads. Those are the tactics, and all those tactics are very learnable, but what's most important about sales is being great at relationship building or willing to learn how to be.

A large percentage of the population is good at that. There are definitely some people who are not. I'm not assuming everybody should be in sales, but if you genuinely enjoy sitting down and having a cup of coffee with someone, hear about their problems, explain how you might be able to help them solve that problem, then you can be excellent at sales. The rest of the sales tools you would need are learnable.

## Talent Versus Hard Work

My business partner, Kelly Roach, says you have to train for business like athletes train for their sport. No swimmer was born an Olympic swimmer. They learned how to swim and once they learned how to swim, they trained. They practiced and they hired coaches and they practiced some more, and they competed and probably lost more swim meets than they won.

It's the exact same thing with any skill, including sales. You can learn the tactics and you can have the ability to connect and build relationships. You get really good at selling because of the practice. The practice includes running the drills. You can run the drills in real life, out in the wild, like talking to people at the grocery store. You can run the drills through role-plays. You could run the drills when hiring a coach, but nobody gets really good at anything by skipping these practice steps.

I think that's such an important part of talent versus hard work. There are people that are naturally talented and then there are the people that actually do the work to learn the skill. I would argue that I would rather have the person who wants to run the reps in practice than just have the person who's talented, but lazy. We all know that person in our life who is so talented, but never lived up to their potential. They are tougher to train.

Whereas we know a lot of people who busted their ass getting where they are today. They learned, did the drills, and they failed over and over again. They made all the mistakes and they put their foot in their mouth and they embarrassed them-selves in conversations. They had sales calls bomb, but they managed to make it work because they kept practicing. They didn't let their failures stop them.

Sales is a learnable skill, but it's not something that you learn once and it's done. It is something that you have to practice and drill and rehearse over and over again. Just like anything else you want to be successful at, you practice. Even if you are natu-rally gifted at relationship building, even if you are naturally gifted at talking to people, you still have to run the drills.

When I worked in sales, I hunted all the time for the silver bullet. I knew when I started a business, I kept looking for the easy button, the magical thing that was all the sudden going to open the floodgates and let all the money flow in.

The problem is that the magic bullet, the easy button, the secret sauce is consistency. There is no magic to it, so you can become frustrated that things aren't happening fast enough. That's because you're not consistent on any one strategy.

Consider this: isn't it cool that we live in a world where there are 1,000,001 different ways to grow a business? And 1,000,001 different ways to sell? And they all work?

There are reasons why we teach our method and somebody else teaches their method, and twelve other people teach their own sales methods. All the sales methods work, all the marketing methods work.

You may think success is due to talent. You think it has to do with personality traits. You think they must know more. Maybe your peers just had more connections than you did. They grew up in an environment where you learn how to sell easily. They went to a certain school, and that made it easier for them to sell. They had a certain level of mentoring.

We think all those things are the easy button, but that's why there are so many rags to riches stories in the world – people who started from nothing and became extremely successful in all walks of life. It all goes back to consistency. When it comes to talent versus hard work, it is the person who shows up consistently and is willing to do it wrong. The person who is willing to be bad, the person who is willing to get rejected repeatedly, will eventually succeed.

Those are the most successful people in sales. If you were to go into a company or talk to entrepreneurs and ask them to name their most successful salesperson, they would name the people who are the most consistent. When it comes to having a skill set, having a personality type, knowing the tactics, and even running the drills, if you are not consistently showing up every single day meeting people, building relationships, and solving problems, it doesn't matter how magically talented you are.

Our brains cannot handle the fact that it could possibly be that easy. All you have to do is keep showing up over and over again. That's it. It's about your activity every single day. It has a compound effect. I always talk about looking at the numbers and how many new people you are talking to. Let's say that number is twenty-five per day over five days per week equals 125 people per week. That's 500 people a month, which is 6,000 people a year, all by talking to just twenty-five people five days a week. Imagine that you were in conversation with 6,000 people, at the rate of 3% of our audience who are at any given time ready to buy, that's 180 hot customers. If you were to consistently talk to twenty-five people every day, this is the outcome you can expect.

The problem is by Day 72, you're bored. You're frustrated. It's not happening fast enough. You get daily promo emails in your inbox about the new, easy button and this new secret sauce and this new program that's going to make running your business easy and make you rich at the same time.

Then you're off to the races, buying the course, taking the challenge, joining a mastermind. The problem that salespeople and business owners alike have is that they're too busy chasing the hottest trendiest tactic and they miss the boring, not so sexy consistency that will bring success.

You see this happen on social media all the time, and maybe this is you? You're trying to be seen and known, maybe even famous, on the latest social media platform for a month or two, and then realize creating that amount of content is a ton of work.

Then you're off to the next thing. It looks like you're consistently working, but you haven't been working any one thing long enough to get the results. No one is immune to this. I know because I teach, train, and make a living off people who are pushing against the idea of consistency. Even I still fight the urge to follow the bright, shiny object.

Anytime you try something new inside any of my companies, we do it for a minimum length of time. In fact, if you are going to try a specific strategy, you have to try this strategy for ninety days. You don't get to do this for a week or two or three because that doesn't offer enough consistency to get any kind of results that show its potential.

I get it. You struggle with ninety days of doing sales so much that you want to pull your hair out. You want to do anything but talk to twenty-five people every day.

Success and mastery come with tons of practice. That's why the 1% is the 1%. That's why the top performers are the top performers. That's why the successful businesses are the most successful – because they are consistently developing mastery, consistently doing the reps, doing the drills, and showing up and practicing the discipline of not deviating from the plan.

Consistency looks different from when I started selling in 2004. The data showed then that you needed to get in front of people seven times to be noticed. When I started a business in 2018, the data showed that twelve to sixteen touches were needed to get someone's attention. The data now shows that the number is somewhere between twenty and fifty touches to be noticed.

The reason for that change is because of the amount of stimulation you are hit with on any one day. You live in a world where everyone is inundated with thousands of different marketing messages, email direct messages, Instagram stories, Tik Tok reels, YouTube videos, podcasts, books, and live video. There's so much information coming at you on any given day that you can't hold an attention span long enough to consume it. In order for you to get people's attention, you have to try harder. You have to be louder.

You have to be more persistent with your outreach. This is another place where hard work beats talent because it doesn't matter if you weren't the best salesperson in the world. If you can't get people to pay attention to you, it doesn't matter if you are an excellent closer who closes deals immediately. Notice that none of these things have anything to do with how good you are or not and nothing to do with your personality type.

Success in business and success in sales is so often about the person who is willing to go the extra mile, the person who is willing to actually have the discipline and the commitment to make those touches and the person who is willing to get over their own thoughts about making it happen because it is super-duper uncomfortable to reach out to somebody twenty times.

You have all the drama in your head about what people think of you. You even ask yourself, *how am I doing? They must think I'm so annoying. They must know what I offer by now. They have to know about my programs. There's no way in the world that they don't know who I am and what I do.*

## Focus on Problem Solving

You may feel uncomfortable continuing to work the system in that way. What we find repeatedly is that most people will ignore you until their problem is big enough and painful enough. And then they tell you they need a solution ASAP.

The person they reached out to for the answer and to solve the problem is the person who has been in front of them the most. You network and meet a couple of people and try to show up in a consistent way. After three months, you're frustrated when you see that one of the people you reached out to once or twice has hired another coach or simply decided to work with another company.

You're frustrated because you had reached out to that person. You had made an offer to that person. The problem is that you were not still in front of that person. The person who got them as a client was. Sure, it seems unfair. It seems like you can't be in front of all the people you've touched in the last three months, enough times that they hire you.

You can get hung up in your drama about outreach and the time it takes to be committed. You're thinking, *she wants me to reach out to twenty-five new people and how am I ever going to get through all these touches on top of running a business and all the other responsibilities that I have?*

Your data tells you to be consistent in your outreach, and your data tells you that the best way to do that is to create familiarity. That's the hard work because everything that we talked about in this chapter has nothing to do with talent, ability, or tactic. It all has to do with consistency and discipline.

Even career sales reps who are excellent and at the top of their game don't find this the favorite part of their job. For you, it's short-term sacrifice for long-term gain. You're going to do the uncomfortable part of your job so that you can wow your clients with amazing results and make as much money as you want to make.

You know, there's nothing in life that comes as easily and allows us to enjoy the fruits of our labor quite like sales. It's probably why I love sales so much. You show up and consistently do the work. It's as systematic as you need it to be.

Let me tell you about how I decided to start working with Kelly Roach, who was my business coach and is now my business partner. I came into Kelly's world in 2018. She had reached out to me on LinkedIn. I got on the phone and had a sales conversation with her, and I told her no because she wanted me to take her course. I just don't do courses, so I said, no, and I hired a different coach.

Kelly's team stayed in front of me. They continued to send me messages, share resources, invite me to events, and have conversations. Even though I was working with someone else and had no interest in the course they offered, they consistently stayed in front of me. Six months later, I became a client, one of their success stories, and then Kelly and I started a business together.

This is an example of consistency, persistence, and discipline. We had a sales conversation and I said no, but they continued to stay in front of me and provide value. They continued to be helpful and ultimately, I joined Kelly's program.

Now think of the lifetime value to me. I didn't stay at their lowest level program. I ascended into the mastermind as well. I was entering my third year of working with them when Kelly and I decided to start a business. Imagine if she thought, *she's not interested in working with us*. And then she stopped contacting me. Now think of the revenue that was brought into Kelly's business and the fact that we started a new business that is on pace to be a seven-figure company in its first year. Think of how much opportunity came out of that persistence and commitment to stay in touch with me.

That is what can happen when you get to know people and you see how to help them out. Then before you know it, you're partnering with them and making millions of dollars as the business grows.

# BONUS
## POWER HOUR HOW-TO

Let's talk about the Power Hour. Whether you're starting your sales career or business, or you've been in sales for a while, the Power Hour is what moves the needle from zero to success for you.

This is the hour that should be on your calendar every single day because it will help you grow your business. Even as your business becomes more successful, even as you get more clients, even as you continue to grow, the Power Hour is super, super magical. So, what is the Power Hour? And why is it important to you?

When I started my business alongside my full-time job, I committed an hour a day to doing the things that would grow my business and eventually help me leave my job.

Yes, you are busy, you're trying to leave your job, too, or you're a mom with small children. But what this hour will do for you cannot be underestimated. I also know that you can come up with an hour a day, and you can even split it up the hour over the day. You do not have to commit to the full hour all at once. I broke my Power Hour into three twenty-minute sections.

My first twenty-minute block is what I called my outbound block. This is where you work on your outbound comments. My second twenty-minute block was my conversations, going back and forth in comments. And then my third block was my direct message block.

The reason why I want you to break this into three separate blocks is because, if you try to do all these things at one time, you will not be successful. I'm gonna say that again. If you try to get the outbound block and the messages back and forth and the direct messages sent all at one time, you will not get enough touch points for this strategy to work for you.

What do I mean by that? Facebook is my jam, but I know that this works on LinkedIn and Instagram, too. I want you to interact, whether it's in groups or the social media feeds, with your potential clients. So, this can look like going into Facebook groups with a lot of potential clients, sorting by most recent posts, and then commenting and interacting with as many posts as possible.

You are not just in there to answer questions. You are not just looking for people who are looking for you. You are answering every single question that you can. If somebody says, "Hey, I'm celebrating, leaving my full-time job," comment with *Congratulations. That's so exciting. What are you doing to celebrate?*

If somebody is asking for help, answer their question. What's key to this is making sure you're not overthinking your answers and making sure you end your answers with a question. Let's use an example. You're a health coach and someone is looking for help with allergies and food sensitivities. You can comment that you have great gluten-free recipes. They write, *my sister-in-law is coming to visit and she's allergic.* And while you are really an expert on weight loss, commenting on the gluten issue gets you noticed and the information you provide is accurate and helpful.

Plus, you're starting a conversation, which is how you build a relationship. You may cite a website with great recipes or ask what meals they are looking for. You are now engaging them in a conversation, and you've asked them a question. Don't over-think all of this. You are just commenting on someone's post to bring awareness about you and to start a conversation.

Make certain that you are not responding to their answer back to you from your first twenty-minute block of your Power Hour. You're just going for outbound touches in this first block. If you do outbound and replies to your questions, you won't get as many outbound touches as you need.

For outbound touches, make as many comments as you can in a set time period, or until you make, say, ten to twenty comments. This is your outbound block. This is 1) meant to create conversations, and 2) meant to keep you visible. If you go into Facebook groups and comment on twenty-five posts, a whole bunch of people are going to see your name and you are going to be seen as someone who is helpful, valuable, and interesting, right?

That's all we're trying to do is get people's attention and start conversations. This outbound block is so important. Most people are not commenting on enough things. They're not getting enough visibility to really have this be effective. So again, set your timer, pick your number of outbound touches and only outbound.

Now, you just went into Facebook and asked a bunch of

questions. That prompts people to start answering you. Go back and continue those conversations. It does us no good to just push the outbound and not continue the conversation. How you get clients is in the human-to-human connection and back and forth conversations.

You want to make sure that you go back and complete the second twenty-minute block. Again, set your timer, decide on a certain number of conversations, whatever works best for you, but just make sure you're moving those conversations forward. My rule of thumb? Once I have gone back and forth with someone one or two times in the comments, I'm moving it to the direct messages.

You are moving it into a person-to-person, one-to-one conversation. I like to view this just as you would at an in-person networking event. When you meet people at an event, you start conversations, and hopefully, with lots of the people there. Then you select certain people that you want to have a one-on-one conversation with. That's what you're doing as you get them into the direct messages (DM), which is the third twenty-minute block of that Power Hour.

It might be as simple as, *hey, Sarah, do you mind if I direct message you a couple of recipes that are favorites in our household?* You've asked for permission, or maybe you just send Sarah a direct message. Also send her a quick friend request if you're on Facebook. When you do say, *we were chatting in this group, and I wanted to send you a couple of gluten-free recipes that are favorites in our house.*

All that you're looking to do is to continue the conversation. You don't yet know if this person is a potential client. You are still just meeting people and having conversations. The questions you may ask could be, *what are some of your favorite foods?*

*Oh, great! You know, I'm a health coach and I help people with this. You can follow me on Instagram, or you can join my Facebook group, or I love to share really great recipes. Would you be interested in me emailing them to you?*

You're inviting people into your circle of influence. If the conversation isn't going anywhere, say, *I love getting to know you,* or something like that, but know that you are managing the direct messages and the direct messages are where you start talking to people on a deeper level.

Ask yourself questions about the person: do they fit the criteria of your ideal client? Do you want to invite them to a connection call or strategy call? Do I want to invite them to a sales call? Do you want to invite them to your Facebook group? Or are they right now just another person who knows what you do so the next time somebody is looking for a nutritionist, they can refer you.

Not every single one of these direct message conversations is going to turn into a sales conversation. That is okay. Remember, sales is not always the point. The more people who know what you do, the greater the chances are that you'll be referred by them or hired by them. You never know who they know. So again, the first twenty-minute block is your outbound touch points. Boom, boom, boom, quickly, then your second block are replies to comments you've already made.

Move the conversation forward one or two comments back and forth, and then move into DMs to continue the conversation. This is just like you were in person. Ask yourself, *if I met this person at a live event, when would it be appropriate to make an invitation for a cup of coffee? When would it be appropriate to invite somebody to a sales conversation? Would it be appropriate to invite someone to my Facebook group?*

If you wouldn't say it in person, do not say it in the DM, but do not overthink the direct message strategy. Will your DMs go crazy with replies? Yes. And as a matter of fact, this is what you call prospecting. You have to be talking to a lot of different people because not all the people are going to be your ideal client, or even accept an invitation to chat with you in direct messages.

The Power Hour is on your calendar for at least every weekday, week in and week out. If you follow this strategy, I promise that you will get opportunities to have conversations with people that are either going to be A) *Oh my gosh, you do that? I need your help with that,* or B) You're going to be able to say, *hey, listen, you mentioned that you needed help. I'm offering you my help.* But know that you have to be super intentional with your time. If this time is not on your calendar every single day, it will be very easy to skip.

The Power Hour is the most powerful thing that you can do inside of your business. This is a practice that supports the relationship building I've talked about throughout this book. Make sure you're having a conversation with enough people to get super visible, and to start building your credibility and authority, which are the keys to success in your service-based business.

As you have figured out by now, being an entrepreneur is not for the faint hearted. The good news is that sales is a definable skill that can be learned. Remember to hustle and flow, use your Power Hour to your advantage, and above all, build relationships. Put all that together with solving real problems for real people within your specific niche, and you will succeed.

Oh, and PS: have some fun with it!